Kieler Studien

Institut für Weltwirtschaft an der Universität Kiel

Herausgegeben von Herbert Giersch

167

Sanjeev Gupta, Ph. D.

Black Market Exchange Rates

J.C.B. MOHR (PAUL SIEBECK) TÜBINGEN

ISSN 0340-6989

CIP-Kurztitelaufnahme der Deutschen Bibliothek

Gupta, Sanjeev:
Black market exchange rates / Sanjeev Gupta. —
Tübingen: Mohr, 1981.
(Kieler Studien; 167)
ISBN 3-16-343991-8 kart.
ISBN 3-16-343992-6 Gewebe
NE: GT

Schriftleitung: Hubertus Müller-Groeling

Printed in Germany
ISSN 0340-6989

To My Parents

Contents

Page

List of Tables

List of Figures

Preface

A black market in foreign exchange usually emerges whenever controls are imposed on the foreign sector of an economy. However, these controls are not fully effective since incentive exists to circumvent them and raise the private returns by smuggling, under- and over-invoicing on legal trade and diversion of remittances. Since many transactions take place at the black market exchange rate, it is an important variable in many economies, influencing the allocation of resources, the level of foreign exchange reserves and the distribution of income. The present study examines the determinants of this exchange rate, the nature of a black market and the question whether it is efficient in the sense that it makes use of the available information in determining the black exchange rate.

This work was originally submitted as a Ph. D. dissertation in economics at Simon Fraser University, Vancouver, in July 1980. It was revised after I joined the Institut für Weltwirtschaft, Kiel.

For helpful comments and suggestions received during the preparation of this study, I am thankful to Phillipe Callier of Concordia University, James Dean, Phillippa Dee, Stephen Easton, Poonam Gupta, Herbert G. Grubel and Edward Tower of Simon Fraser University, John Heaney of University of British Columbia and Hans Stoll of Wharton School, University of Pennsylvania. In addition, I have benefited from discussions with J. B. Donges, H. Müller-Groeling and other colleagues at the Institut für Weltwirtschaft. Thanks are also due to Ursula Wollesen who has taken care of the editorial work.

Sections of this study have appeared in the Journal of Finance, Vol. 36, and Weltwirtschaftliches Archiv, Vol. 116.

Kiel, June 1981 Sanjeev Gupta

I. Introduction

A price ceiling, with or without rationing, is likely to give rise to a black market. In such a market, the commodities are sold illegally at a price that is above the officially permitted price. The central authorities set the price that producers receive for their product, which is below the free-market price. This lowers the quantity supplied to the market. However, at the retail level, this price control is difficult to enforce and the opportunity for a black market emerges. It pays black market participants to buy at the controlled price and sell at the (higher) black market price. Since goods are in short supply, the consumers willingly pay a higher price than the government set ceiling price.

There is ample evidence that an effective price ceiling is usually accompanied by the emergence of a black market. During World War I and World War II, major belligerent powers instituted schemes that set the prices of many food items below the free-market equilibrium prices. These schemes led to shortages and to the establishment of a black market. Tight market conditions were reflected in the institution of "trekking" which developed in a number of countries. City dwellers searched the nearby countryside for food, making private black market deals with the farmers. The more the governments succeeded in controlling the prices of foodstuffs in the official market, the more the system of trekking flourished[1].

The existence and operation of the black market has not escaped the attention of researchers. Boulding [1947], Bronfenbrenner [1947] and Michaely [1954] have analysed theoretically the operation of this market for a single commodity[2]. Only recently, however, have models for the analysis

---

[1] For instance, see Cohen [1949, p. 378]. - In recent times, minimum wage laws, rent controls and various price support programmes may be cited as instances of intervention by authorities in the free operation of the price mechanism.

[2] A simple analysis of black markets can also be found in the price theory textbooks. See, for example Hirshleifer [1976, Ch. 2] and Layard, Walters [1978, Ch. 6].

of black markets in foreign currencies been developed, partly because of a better understanding of the black markets by the academics and partly because of the greater availability and accuracy of data[1]. These markets are a consequence of controls imposed on the foreign sector by some, but especially the developing countries[2]. The restrictions on the foreign sector take the form of tariffs and quotas on goods, controls on capital flows and foreign exchange transactions[3]. These regulations lead to smuggling, illegal capital flows and to the establishment of a black market in foreign currencies to finance the illegal imports and exports of goods and assets. Controls on the foreign sector are popular with developing countries despite associated undesirable effects. This popularity of controls stems from the fact that they are considered to be a part of the overall development plans and also because there exists a general distrust in the ability of the free market to lead to socially optimal production and income patterns.

A "high" premium on the foreign currencies usually exists in countries where restrictions on the foreign sector have been imposed. The factors that contribute to a premium are the severity of the restrictions and the general economic conditions prevailing in the home economy which lead to the creation of an excess demand in many commodities and markets.

This study of black markets in foreign currencies has been stimulated by, first, the availability of a new theory of exchange rate determination, popularly known as the "monetarist" theory[4]. Second, adequate data on black market exchange rates is now readily available to test new and existing theories in international trade and finance. The data on monthly series of exchange rates for almost all countries with re-

---

[1] For example, see Culbertson [1975], Sheikh [1976], Blejer [1978], Fishelson [1978] and Giddy [1978a].

[2] For a detailed discussion on exchange controls and restrictions on foreign trade in the developing countries, see Little et al. [1970, Ch. 2, 6].

[3] For a brief exposition of controls on the foreign trade sector, see Grubel [1977, Ch. 15].

[4] In the monetarist models, the exchange rate is determined by the conditions of stock equilibrium and by the interaction of goods and money markets. For details, see Frenkel [1976] and Dornbusch [1976a; 1976b].

strictions on the foreign sector can be obtained from the various issues of the Pick's Currency Yearbook. From 1976 onwards, weekly data for some Asian and Far Eastern countries is published on a regular basis in the Far Eastern Economic Review.

Third, an understanding of determinants of the black market in foreign exchange continues to be of great interest to policy makers, because the number of transactions that take place at this exchange rate make it an important variable in the economy of many countries, influencing the allocation of resources, the achievement of plan objectives, level of foreign exchange reserves and distribution of income.

Since the black market rate influences the level of foreign exchange reserves, it is useful to spell out more fully the relationship between the two. An increase in the black market rate, given the official rate, has the following effects:

(1) It creates incentive for residents abroad to channel their remittances through the black market, as this raises their private receipts in terms of home currency. As a result, the central bank is deprived of this foreign exchange. This is particularly relevant for some of the developing countries, like India, which have emerged as major exporters of skilled and unskilled manpower.

(2) It creates incentive to smuggle and under-invoice exports. This incentive exists under three conditions:

- First, when there is a premium[1] on foreign currencies with no tariff or subsidy on the exports. Under these circumstances, the sale of foreign exchange in the black market increases the receipts of the exporter in terms of home currency;
- second, when there is a tariff on exports, under-invoicing permits the exporter to avoid the tariff and to sell the illegally acquired foreign exchange at a premium;
- third, when there is a subsidy on exports which is less than the black market premium on the foreign exchange. The

---

[1] This premium is expressed as a percentage of the official rate.

sale of foreign exchange at a premium more than compensates for the loss of subsidy[1].

(3) It reduces incentive to over-invoice exports. An incentive to over-invoice exports exists whenever the subsidy is greater than the premium. This is because the subsidy obtained on the over-invoiced part of exports more than offsets the premium that needs to be paid in buying foreign exchange in the black market.

The effect of (1) and (2) on the balance of payments is to lower the official foreign exchange receipts of the country. However, the over-invoicing of exports tends to have a favourable effect on the balance of payments[2].

The effect of the black market in foreign currencies on the reserve flow can be analysed more rigorously through the following model:

$$dR/dt = X - M - Xb$$

where

R = foreign exchange reserves

X = export receipts in foreign currency (say, \$)

M = the level of imports permitted by the authorities (\$)

Xb = that part of the export receipts and remittances that is diverted to the black market for foreign exchange, where $Xb = f\,(1/Eo - 1/Eb)$, with $1/Eo - 1/Eb \geq 0$, Eo being the official price and Eb the black market price of one unit of foreign currency in terms of domestic currency

---

[1] It should be noted that under-invoicing of exports can occur in spite of tariff and subsidy policies of a country. One such case and evidence in its favour is discussed by Bhagwati, Krueger and Wibulswasdi in Bhagwati [1974].

[2] For a detailed discussion on under-invoicing and over-invoicing of exports and its economic effects on the balance of payments, see Bhagwati [1967].

Because of the factors discussed above, diversion of export receipts and remittances to the black market would be larger, the higher the premium on foreign currencies. Thus,

$$f' > 0$$

$$d^2 R/dt\, d(1/Eo - 1/Eb) < 0$$

Therefore, changes in reserve holdings are seen to be a function of official and black market exchange rates. Since most of the developing countries suffer from a shortage of foreign exchange, it is in their interest to keep the black market rate as low as possible by influencing the determinants of the black market exchange rate. By doing this, they can gain foreign exchange reserves.

Further, under-invoicing and over-invoicing of transactions on legal trade affects the composition of the balance of payments. This not only misleads the policy makers of the country who base their analysis on trends in the balance of payments, but also affects the aid flows and thus the reserve position of the country. The aid inflows are partly influenced by the foreign exchange position of the recipient country. An indication of the fact that the recipient country can eventually earn enough foreign exchange to pay for its imports and meet its debt servicing requirements creates a healthy impression on the aid donors[1].

Lastly, it is of interest to the students of international economics and finance to investigate whether the black markets in foreign currencies process the available information efficiently. Given that these markets are characterised by a lack of complete information about prices and participants, and are often thin and segmented, the relevant empirical question is whether the exchange rates in these markets adjust to all the new information. If the exchange rate in this market reflects the available information, it would be interesting to see if the black market anticipates changes in the official exchange rate. That is, whether the movements in the black market exchange rate "forecast" movements in the official rate.

---

[1] For details, see Bhagwati [1967].

Therefore, the contribution of this study lies (a) in improving upon the existing models on the determinants of black market in foreign currencies in light of a "new" theory of exchange rate determination, (b) in providing evidence in support of this "improved" model, (c) in applying the various tests of market efficiency on the black market exchange rate series of some countries, (d) in reporting the results that have important and interesting policy implications.

I intend to study the nature of black markets in foreign exchange by discussing the following topics:

In Chapter I, I have discussed the conditions under which black markets for foreign exchange develop and why a study of the determinants of the black market rates is of theoretical and practical interest.

In Chapter II, I analyse the nature of these markets in terms of partial equilibrium demand and supply apparatus, present estimates of under- und over-invoicing on legal trade and smuggling in India, and review the existing models and empirical work to highlight the deficiencies in them.

Chapter III formally develops a model for the determinants of the black market in foreign exchange by making use of the "monetarist" assumptions. The variables of the model are expressed in terms of empirical proxies and the model's parameters then estimated for India.

In Chapter IV, I summarise various models that have been used to test for efficiency of the freely floating exchange rates in the weak form sense, and use one of them to explore whether black markets in foreign currencies for India, South Korea and Taiwan are efficient processors of the publicly available information. In addition, the cross-correlations between the changes in the black market rate and changes in the official exchange rate are examined to see if the black market exchange rate "predicts" the movements in the official rate.

Chapter V, summarises the findings and advances policy implications.

II. The Nature of Black Markets

In this chapter, I first discuss reasons for the emergence of a black market in commodities. These factors are then incorporated into a partial equilibrium model of black markets in foreign currencies. In this model, I distinguish two sources of supply of foreign exchange to the black market: the resale of officially allocated foreign exchange and foreign exchange obtained through under-invoicing and smuggling of exports. In addition, the model allows for the effect on the behaviour of participants and the price of foreign exchange of penalties for dealing in black market currencies. It is shown that if penalties are severe enough, the black market exchange rate can lie below the free market exchange rate.

In the following section, I present estimates of misreporting on legal trade and smuggling for India, based on a government committee report, 'educated guesses' and other independent studies. I then relate the estimates of under-invoicing on exports and imports, and smuggling to total legal trade, to put these estimates into a proper perspective. The mechanics of how the residents living abroad remit their earnings through the black market is described in the succeeding section.

In the last section, I present a critical survey of the existing models on the determinants of black market exchange rate. The primary objective is to bring out the inherent deficiencies. A model is then developed in the succeeding chapter which attempts to overcome these shortcomings in a framework with less restrictive assumptions.

1. What is a Black Market?

There are many ways to allocate private goods of which the best known is the price mechanism. However, in many economies, free bargaining of the price mechanism has been abrogated in favour of non-price allocation systems. In these systems, an excess demand in the market is not eliminated by a rise in the price level. Instead, the available supply of commodities is allocated to the consumers by methods whose exact nature is determined by the authorities. An allocation method must be distinguished from an allocation criterion. The latter implies a standard on which a judgement may be based. The various allocation methods can be assessed from the point of view of costs and benefits both to the consumer and to the allocator.

Some of the best known allocation methods are,

(1) Queueing: The commodities are sold on a 'first come, first serve' basis. Hence, the buyer has to spend a certain amount of time in the queue to buy a specific quantity of the good and service. The cost to the consumer is in terms of the opportunity cost of time and foregone earnings. If w is the wage rate and t is the time spent in the queue, then wt is the direct cost to the consumer in addition to the money price of the commodity. The advantage of this system lies in that no administrative criteria are needed. Thus, the monetary and organisational costs are avoided. The benefit to the consumer arises from the fact that the allocation of goods is independent of the personal whims of the allocator.

(2) Administrative Rationing: Here, the individual is allocated a particular quantity of a good. The allotment may be the same for all individuals, or it could be based on some administrative assessment of need. The problem with this system is that the criteria for allocation are not very clearly specified. Their ad hoc nature results in the consumer allocations being determined in large part by the government appointed rationeer. Thus, the consumer could end up spending considerable time and money bribing the rationeer for larger allocations of the scarce commodity. The benefit to the consumer, however, lies in the savings from not having to stand in long queues.

A black market emerges whenever there is an excess demand resulting from a price ceiling. The allocation of goods via queueing and administrative rationing may not be acceptable to all consumers some of whom may still prefer to transact in the black market. I discussed above that there is an opportunity cost of queueing. The higher the wage rate, the greater would be the unwillingness to stand in queues. Hence, people with high wage rates would prefer to buy at the black market price rather than stand in a queue. In the rationing system, coupons are usually distributed for the purchase of a fixed quantity of the scarce commodity. Some people with low incomes who cannot afford to purchase the commodity even at the ceiling price, have an incentive to trade their coupons at black market prices. There are gains to be had for both the seller and the buyer by trading in the black market.

These gains from trading in the black market for commodities also exist in the black foreign exchange markets where the official exchange rate is pegged below the equilibrium and there are controls in dealings in the foreign currencies[1]. The excess demand for foreign exchange is dealt with through an elaborate system of controls on how importers can obtain and exporters can use foreign exchange. Thus, exporters (and other earners and recipients of foreign currencies) are required to sell all or most of their foreign currency receipts to the exchange authorities at a specified rate, which is below the equilibrium rate. These receipts are then disbursed to the licenced importers at or near the official rate, with importers required to show full proof of expenditure on imports. But these controls on dealings in foreign exchange are not fully effective since incentives exist to cheat and raise the private returns from exporting and lower the cost of importing. This cheating takes the form of

- smuggling,
- invoicing,
- diversion of remittances.

The above analysis can be illustrated with the help of partial equilibrium demand and supply apparatus. Consider the de-

[1] The overvaluation of the exchange rate is not a necessary condition for the emergence of the black market in foreign currencies. The authorities could auction the limited supply of foreign exchange and capture all the rents. Furthermore, the official exchange rate could be undervalued and a black market for foreign currencies could still exist if the exchange authorities, instead of disbursing the export receipts to the residents of the home country for expenditure on foreign goods, turn them into official reserves. For an example, see Culbertson [1975, fn. 4].

mand-supply diagram of Figure 1. The horizontal axis represents the quantity of foreign exchange per unit of time while the vertical axis measures the price of foreign exchange in terms of domestic currency. Let OR denote the official exchange rate which is below the free market "equilibrium" rate. At this official rate, the quantity supplied by the exporters and other private individuals to the government is OT and the quantity demanded is OT'.

Figure 1 - The Black Foreign Exchange Market: Resale Only

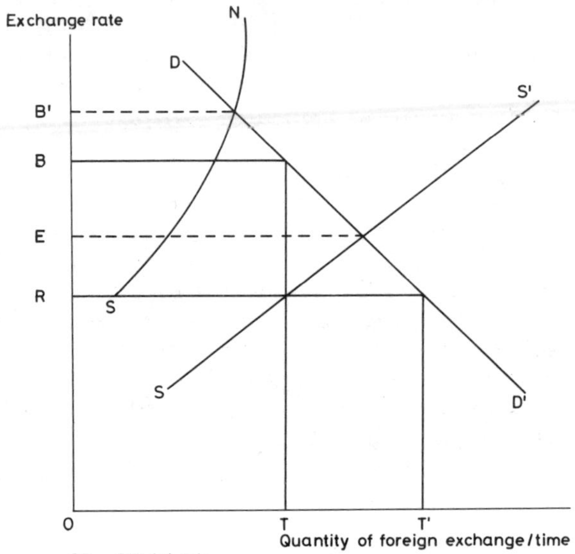

OR = Official rate
OB = Black market rate
DD' = Free market demand for foreign exchange
SS' = Free market supply of foreign exchange
SN = Resale supply of black foreign exchange

Let us first consider the supply side of the market. The foreign exchange supplied to the black market comes either from

(1) the resale of the officially allocated foreign exchange, (for instance, through the over-invoicing of imports), and/or from

(2) the failure to return to the central bank all the revenue because of under-invoicing and smuggling of exports and diversion of remittances.

Source (1) has been stressed by Culbertson and source (2) by Sheikh and Blejer.

If all the officially allocated foreign exchange OT is sold in the black market, then the black market exchange rate would be OB as shown in Figure 1. However, in the real world only a fraction of this potential supply actually shows up in the black market due to fear of prosecution. Under these conditions, the black market supply curve (which has been termed as "resold foreign exchange" supply curve by Giddy [1978a, p. 6] lies to the left of the free market supply curve; it is denoted by SN. The vertical distance between SN and SS' at any point represents the market price of risk for a given penalty structure. For no penalties, SN coincides with SS'. The more severe the penalties, the further to the left lies the SN curve.

The SN curve in Figure 1 is drawn steeper than SS'. This is because an increase in the black market exchange rate brings in a smaller increase in the total supply of foreign exchange through the resale of officially allocated foreign exchange as compared to an increase in foreign exchange supply when the official rate increases. The sellers of the officially allocated exchange add the risk of getting caught to the cost of supplying foreign exchange, thereby supplying smaller quantities at higher black market exchange rates.

Analogously, if foreign exchange receipts obtained through smuggling, under-invoicing and remittances are the only sources of supply of foreign exchange to the black market, then in the absence of penalties, the black market exchange rate is OB_0 in Figure 2. With penalties, the supply curve lies to the left of SS'; it is denoted by SM. (Giddy has termed it as "direct supply" curve). As in the previous case, the vertical distance between SM and SS' at any point represents the market price of risk for a given penalty structure.

Given the official pegged exchange rate, the supply curve of the black market (SM in Figure 2) is drawn steeper than SS'. This is because an increase in the black market rate brings in a lesser increase in the total supply of foreign exchange by increased export of goods and services as compared to an increase in foreign exchange supply when the legal rate in-

Figure 2 - The Black Foreign Exchange Market: Direct Supply Only

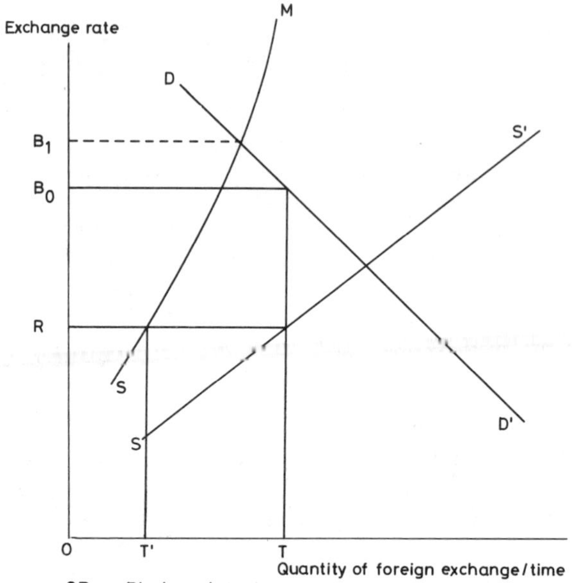

OB_0 - Black market rate
OR = Official rate
SM - Direct supply of black foreign exchange

creases. The exporters add the risk of prosecution to the cost of supplying exportables and hence export less at a given black market rate as compared to the same official rate.

But in reality, the supply of black foreign exchange originates from both sources. Thus, (1) and (2) could be added to get a 'total' black market supply curve SB, as shown in Figure 3. This 'total' is not simply the sum of SN and SM. Under-invoicing, smuggling and the diversion of remittances reduces the foreign exchange receipts of the central bank to OT' (Figure 2). This, in turn, lowers the amount that the central bank has available for allocation to the rationed importers, thus reducing the amount that can be resold in the black market. In addition, the location of the black market supply curve (SB) depends on the differential between the official and the free market exchange rate. The closer the official rate (OR) to the free market rate (OE), the smaller the discrepancy between the black market and the official rate.

Figure 3 - The Black Foreign Exchange Market: Both Resale and Direct Supply

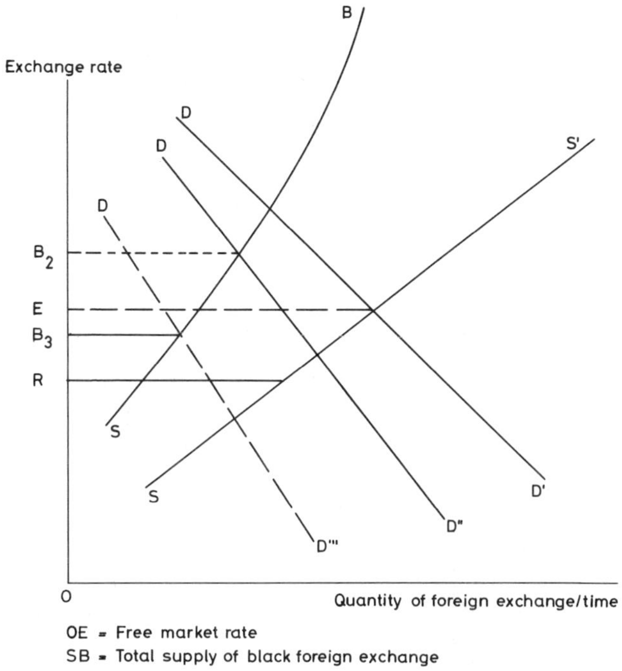

Until now, my concern had been with the supply of foreign exchange to the black market. Now I turn to examine the demand aspect. Foreign exchange in the black market is demanded for the smuggling of goods and assets into the country and for travel abroad. In addition, importers who under-invoice imports demand foreign exchange to pay to the foreign seller the difference between the actual and the invoiced price. Similarly, black foreign exchange is demanded by exporters who over-invoice exports. As the buyers of foreign exchange in the black market are also subject to the risk of prosecution, the black market demand curve lies to the left of the free market demand curve. In Figure 3 the effective black market demand curve is shown as DD" and the emerging black market exchange rate is OB_2. Thus, the location of both the demand and the supply curve is influenced by the penalty structure.

It is possible that the buyers are subject to more severe penalties than the sellers. In that case, the position of the black market demand curve could be DD''' and the resulting black market exchange rate could lie below the free market exchange rate OR, as shown in Figure 3. But this is unlikely since purchaser-penalties are more difficult to enforce by the authorities than penalties imposed on people to whom the foreign exchange is officially allocated. This is because the enforcement agencies have records of all the people who are allocated foreign exchange which makes enforcement easy. However, the authorities have no information or records with which to apprehend the purchasers of black foreign exchange. Under these conditions, the cost of administering purchaser-penalties is higher.

Now I introduce a distinction between smuggling and a black market in foreign exchange which I did not make explicit up to this point. Smuggling does not necessarily lead to a black market in foreign exchange. For instance, tariffs with no controls on the foreign exchange market create incentive for people to smuggle goods across the border without declaring them to the authorities, but do not cause a black market in foreign exchange to emerge because the free market in foreign exchange absorbs all the excess demands and supplies of foreign exchange. Therefore, black markets and smuggling are expected to coexist when there are both exchange controls and tariffs.

Further, it is possible that, even when the foreign exchange market is free from exchange controls, a black market in foreign exchange may exist. This could happen when recording of exchange transactions embarasses the smugglers and other transferers of funds abroad, so that to preserve anonymity, they prefer to deal in the black market. This embarassment may also be due to attempts to avoid income taxes or other levies.

So far the discussion was concerned with theoretical issues. In the following section, I give some estimates that indicate the size of the black market in foreign exchange in India.

2. Estimates of Misreporting on Legal Trade and Smuggling

On the recommendation of the Estimates Committee of Parliament, the Government of India appointed a team in November 1969 to study the problem of under- and over-invoicing on legal trade and smuggling. This committee submitted its report in June 1971 which came to be known as the Kaul Committee Report.

In its report, the Kaul Committee estimated that the total demand for unauthorised foreign exchange was about Rs 2,400 million in 1969. This black foreign exchange was demanded for smuggling of goods into India, foreign travel and for financing under-invoicing of imports and over-invoicing of exports.

A fraction of this demand was met by the smuggling of goods out of India and the sale of foreign exchange by tourists. The committee also noted that 70 per cent of smuggling into India was financed by diversion of remittances to the black market by residents living abroad. The remainder was accounted for by under-invoicing of exports and over-invoicing of imports[1]. A summary of these statistics is presented in Table 1.

Table 1 - Estimates of Black Foreign Exchange for 1969 (million Rs)

Source	Black Foreign Exchange	
	demand	supply
Smuggling	1,600-1,700	400- 500
Travel	350- 450	150
Remittances	-	1,000-1,200
Under- and over-invoicing	250- 300	600- 700
Total	2,200-2,450	2,150-2,500

Source: Kaul Committee Report [1971].

[1] For details, see the Kaul Committee Report [1971, pp. 8-13].

These estimates were not based on any systematic technique of estimation. They were more in the nature of 'educated guesses' and hence were subject to wide margins of error. Nayak [1977; 1979] and Pitre [1978] attempted to improve them by using a more sophisticated procedure which involved a comparison of the trade data of India with that of its trading partners, a technique that had earlier been used by Bhagwati [1964] to study the phenomenon of under-invoicing of imports in Turkey[1].

Nayak's estimates of under- and over-invoicing of exports and imports are presented in Tables 2 and 3, respectively[2]. The negative sign indicates under-invoicing while the positive sign indicates over-invoicing. The estimates presented are only for nine countries which in 1971 constituted 58.5 and 48.6 per cent of India's imports and exports, respectively.

Tables 2 and 3 suggest that more of India's exports and imports are under-invoiced than over-invoiced. Further, misreporting on official exports and imports is most noticeable in trade with Japan, the United States, West Germany and the United Kingdom.

However, I would like to point out that both Nayak and Pitre implicitly assume that the partner-country analysis measures only under- and over-invoicing on legal trade. This is not entirely true. The differences in the official trade statistics of a given country with its trading partners could also be due to smuggling of goods and assets into and out of a country [Naya, Morgan, 1974; Simkin, 1970]. But in the case of India, most of the smuggling takes place around its coastline and the goods are smuggled into and out of the adjoining Middle East countries, presumably because of transport costs[3]. These countries are not included in Nayak and Pitre's sample. Therefore, the estimates in Tables 2 through 4 can

[1] Bhagwati found that Turkey's imports were undervalued as compared to her partner-country's exports for the commodities enjoying high tariff protection.

[2] In his initial calculations, Nayak made some errors which were later corrected by Pitre [1978, Tables 1 and 2]. Tables 2 and 3 here report the corrected estimates.

[3] For a more detailed description of smuggling operations, see the various issues of the Pick's Currency Yearbook.

be taken to represent predominantly the under- and over-invoicing on legal trade rather than smuggling.

By comparing Tables 1 and 4, it can be seen that Nayak's estimates for 1969 are nearly twice those of the Kaul Committee's. Further, Table 4 also suggests that under-invoicing of exports as a proportion of the official exports and under-invoicing of imports as a proportion of the official imports are both significant. This is interesting especially when account is taken of the fact that these estimates are restricted to only nine countries constituting about 50 per cent of the official trade.

The partner-country analysis used by Nayak and Pitre has several weaknesses:

First, while the data on exports is valued at f. o. b. prices, that on imports is valued at c. i. f. so that the figures need to be adjusted for insurance and freight to get comparable figures for exports and imports. Wherever statistics in f. o. b. or c. i. f. are not available, a 10 per cent margin of adjustment has been used. However, to the extent that this margin overestimates insurance and freight, an underestimation of under- and over-invoicing on legal trade results.

Second, errors in the classification of commodities in accordance with SITC (Standard International Trade Classification) code bias the results[1]. This occurs when the countries involved make errors in classifying the traded commodities.

Third, inevitable lags between the shipment of goods and their arrival in the importing country give rise to goods being recorded as 'exported' to a country but not as 'imported' by it. When imports are rising, this understates imports.

Fourth, the above estimates assume that when misreporting occurs at one end, the trader at the other end is unaware of it and does not adjust his reporting accordingly. However, if there is collusion between the importer and the exporter, the above estimates get biased because official trade statistics of the partner-country do not contain these transactions.

Notwithstanding the above problems associated with partner-country analysis, these estimates do serve to indicate the

[1] Bhagwati [1964] reported these errors for Turkey.

Table 2 - Estimates of Over- and Under-Invoicing of India's Exports, 1962-1971 (million U.S. $)

Year	United States	United Kingdom	West Germany	France	Japan	Switzer-land	Belgium	Australia	Italy
1962	-24.00	-12.89	-32.36	- 4.77	-45.92	-13.60	-4.85	+4.52	- 5.90
1963	-21.80	+ 4.94	-17.52	- 6.36	-32.20	- 8.75	-0.64	+1.78	+ 0.99
1964	+ 8.00	- 1.03	-21.42	- 3.36	-31.07	- 3.16	-1.89	+3.94	- 4.56
1965	-38.00	-15.22	-15.95	- 5.26	-50.69	- 2.65	-2.07	-2.06	-32.04
1966	-17.70	- 37.31	-15.06	- 4.90	-49.56	- 3.62	-2.47	+0.65	-23.73
1967	-24.93	- 2.30	-15.07	- 7.51	-57.61	- 3.69	+0.30	+0.73	+ 1.14
1968	-19.30	-13.15	-13.32	- 7.86	-65.06	- 3.49	+1.28	+0.51	+ 4.07
1969	-18.45	-18.40	-19.32	-12.10	-68.23	- 4.22	-1.80	+0.31	- 7.20
1970	-24.76	+ 6.94	-20.00	-12.00	-73.26	- 2.32	-3.20	+1.87	- 8.27
1971	+21.45	-26.65	-21.11	-14.73	-98.04	- 1.92	-2.01	+2.51	- 2.07

Source: Pitre [1978, Table 1].

Table 3 - Estimates of Over- and Under-Invoicing of India's Imports, 1962-1971 (million U.S. $)

Year	United States	United Kingdom	West Germany	Japan	Italy	Canada	Belgium	Switzer-land
1962	- 46.96	+26.54	+ 3.30	-10.85	- 2.04	- 1.50	+ 0.14	-12.13
1963	- 72.38	-40.82	+ 0.53	-31.98	+ 7.62	+ 0.64	- 7.44	-11.11
1964	- 90.10	-37.32	+ 3.48	-55.36	+10.50	-11.36	- 5.78	-17.32
1965	- 46.11	-28.30	+10.55	-49.37	- 1.20	-12.53	-11.98	-15.93
1966	+ 7.76	-64.32	-51.88	-30.09	- 8.45	- 2.11	-12.67	- 1.93
1967	+ 15.22	-30.16	- 5.76	-10.44	- 1.90	- 0.97	-14.86	- 4.24
1968	+ 84.49	- 9.55	+13.42	+12.78	- 8.50	+ 8.22	-25.13	-10.52
1969	+ 44.00	-17.20	-23.73	-14.90	- 0.15	+ 5.07	-33.98	- 8.87
1970	- 21.55	-25.24	-36.01	-16.60	- 3.27	+ 8.94	-32.52	- 7.99
1971	-157.04	-56.47	-42.39	-28.24	- 0.91	-24.67	- 2.76	-12.40

Source: Pitre [1978, Table 2].

Table 4 - Over- and Under-Invoicing as a Proportion of India's Official Trade, 1962-1971 (million Rs)

Year	Exports		Imports		Under-invoicing	Over-invoicing	Under-invoicing	Over-invoicing
	under-invoicing	over-invoicing	under-invoicing	over-invoicing	of exports as per cent of official exports		of imports as per cent of official imports	
1962	686.88	23.85	343.44	147.87	8.23	0.29	2.84	1.20
1963	414.99	38.16	782.28	42.93	4.21	0.39	5.74	0.32
1964	319.59	57.24	1,035.09	66.78	3.15	0.56	6.78	0.44
1965	782.28	-	787.05	52.47	8.39	-	5.38	0.36
1966	950.18[a]	6.17[a]	1,048.90[a]	49.36[a]	7.17	0.05	4.96	0.23
1967	847.84	7.57	514.76	113.55	5.62	0.05	2.34	0.52
1968	923.54	45.42	408.78	900.83	5.78	0.28	2.15	4.74
1969	1,135.50	-	749.43	370.93	7.00	-	4.30	2.12
1970	1,090.08	68.13	1,082.51	68.13	6.65	0.42	5.70	0.36
1971	1,264.19	181.68	2,498.10	7.57	7.10	1.00	11.50	0.03

[a] The official exchange rate was devalued in July 1966 from Rs 4.77 per U.S. dollar to Rs 7.57. Therefore, the trade figures are valued at the former rate in the first half of 1966 and at the latter rate in the second half.

Source: Official trade data obtained from IMF [International Financial Statistics, various years].

extent of under- and over-invoicing on legal trade in India[1].

In Chapter I, I pointed out that under-invoicing of exports occurs when the subsidy on exports is less than the black market premium, or when there are tariffs on exports coupled with a premium on the foreign currencies. Thus it appears that the tariff/subsidy policy on exports in India is such that in the presence of a black market in foreign exchange, an incentive is created to under-invoice exports. Similarly, the tariff structure on imports is such that the tariff rate is greater than the premium on the foreign exchange so that there is a tendency to under-invoice imports.

As Table 4 predominantly represents the under- and over-invoicing on legal trade, Table 5 gives the estimates of smuggling of goods and assets into India. The items included in these estimates are gold, watches, synthetic fibres, synthetic yarn, diamonds and precious stones. Nayak computed the estimates of smuggling of goods and assets into India by first obtaining information on the value of goods seized by the custom authorities. He found that on the average custom authorities are able to seize approximately 10 per cent of the total contraband every year[2]. Additional support for this figure was obtained from the fact that smugglers insure against risk of seizure by buying insurance sold by an unauthorized organisation. The premium for this insurance is about 17 per cent of the total value of the contraband. This suggests that 17 per cent insurance premium covers the 10 per cent probability of seizure for the insurance "company" and the remaining seven per cent constitute the operating expenses.

The estimates of smuggling into India in Table 5 are then obtained by multiplying the value of contraband seized by ten[3]. These estimates indicate that smuggling as a proportion of official imports has been significant in the seventies.

Some estimates of gold smuggling obtained from other sources suggest that Table 5 understates the extent of smug-

---

[1] For instance, see Bhagwati [1964] and Naya, Morgan [1974].

[2] This can also be seen from the various issues of Pick's Currency Yearbook.

[3] For a detailed description of the goods seized by the customs authorities, see Nayak [1977, pp. 2057 f.].

Table 5 - Smuggled Goods and Assets as a Proportion of India's Official Imports, 1961-1974

Year	Smuggled Goods and Assets		Year	Smuggled Goods and Assets	
	value in million Rs	as a proportion of total official imports		value in million Rs	as a proportion of total official imports
1961	475	4.32	1968	2,108	11.11
1962	592	4.90	1969	2,506	14.35
1963	359	2.63	1970	2,217	11.16
1964	413	2.71	1971	2,082	9.59
1965	454	3.10	1972	2,444	10.50
1966	507	2.40	1973	3,548	12.00
1967	1,977	8.98	1974	5,763	11.90

Source: Pitre [1978, Table 5]. - Figures for the official imports obtained from IMF [International Financial Statistics, various years].

gling into India. For instance, it has been estimated that the gold smuggled into India has ranged from 10 tons a month [Pick's Currency Yearbook, 1975/76, p. 700] to about 200 tons a year [White, Stanfield, 1974, p. 40]. The value of these 'imports' has varied between $ 200 million and $ 300 million a year in the early seventies. At the official exchange rate (Rs 7.58 per U.S. dollar) in 1972, the value of this smuggled gold alone lay between Rs 1.5 billion and Rs 2.275 billion a year, which is approximately 6 to 10 per cent of the total official imports in that year[1]. Hence, smuggling of gold alone matches the estimates of Table 5 for the early seventies.

3. The Mechanics of Black Market Remittances

A considerable number of Indians are living in Far East, Western Asia, Western Europe and North America. Many of these Indians regularly remit money to their family members or close relatives living in India. Since there is usually a premium on foreign currencies, there exists a strong incentive for Indians remitting money to do so through the black market. As discussed in the previous sections of this chapter, this market is fairly well developed.

The use of the black market has not only increased the private pecuniary return of the remitter but has also provided many nonpecuniary benefits, thereby raising the overall return. The nonpecuniary benefits have taken the form of shorter delivery periods, and avoidance of numerous bureaucratic controls and red tape that is associated with sending money through the official channels. The intermediary hired by the remitter also ensures delivery of funds in cash at the residence of the recipient. The latter is particularly relevant for people living in the villages who may not have ready access to a bank. Even where banking facilities are available, possible illiteracy of the recipient or his distrust of banks may be a hindrance to the transaction.

In countries where the density of Indian population is relatively high, many agencies have cropped up providing the

[1] The total official imports in 1972 were Rs 23.28 billion.

"remittance services." The foreign exchange is collected by these agencies from the remitters and then sold at the black market price to individuals desiring to under-invoice exports and/or imports, to smuggle goods and assets into India, and to pay for personal travel. In this way, these agencies are intermediaries between the demanders and the sellers of black foreign exchange.

It is worth noting that a minimal use of legal channels is made in the remittance operation. Banking services are generally not used for fear of detection by the authorities. The intermediary sends coded messages to his representative in India, giving the list of people to whom the money is to be delivered. Telegrams and letters contain messages that read as "Give this medicine to Mr. X of ." or "Give one sweater to Mr. Y." These codes make it difficult for the Indian authorities to prosecute the individuals involved. At times, the coded letters are sent through a traveller visiting India who then either delivers or mails it to the agent's representative. This is made easier for those agencies that run a travel business along with "remittance services."

Most of the remittances flow to the rural areas. Since the agricultural incomes are not taxed in India, the recipient does not have to declare the flow of cash to the authorities[1].

4. A Critical Survey of the Models

The first attempt to study black markets in foreign currencies and their determinants was made by Culbertson [1975]. He used partial equilibrium demand-supply apparatus to analyse the effects of changes in domestic prices, official exchange rate and foreign exchange reserves on the black market exchange rate.

The purchasing-power-parity doctrine asserts that changes in relative price levels to a large extent dominate changes in the equilibrium (or the market clearing) exchange rate. Therefore, in an economy where the official exchange rate

---

[1] For a case study on the impact of foreign remittances on an Indian village, see Prakash [1978].

is pegged below the equilibrium exchange rate, a correspondence is likely to exist between movements in the latter and the black market exchange rate, provided the official exchange rate and penalty structure do not change. This is because an increase in the domestic price level relative to the foreign price level causes the purchasing-power-parity rate to change, resulting in shifts of the demand and supply schedules of foreign exchange. With no corresponding change in other factors, the gap between the official and the black market exchange rate tends to widen[1].

On this basis, Culbertson employs black market exchange rates in a test of the purchasing-power-parity theory. Thus, in his model, a change in the market clearing rate induced by relatively higher home country inflation would be expected to have a significant effect on the black market exchange rate. Further, since the main source of supply to the black market is assumed to be the resale of the officially allocated foreign exchange, a change in the official rate tends to increase the supply of foreign exchange to the black market through higher export receipts[2]. Therefore, the official rate is the second factor that influences the black market exchange rate. Finally, the black market exchange rate is to some extent influenced by changes in the official reserves, since part of the excess demand in the black market can be satisfied by drawing down the stock of reserves.

Culbertson empirically tested the above model with its three principal determinants of the black market exchange rate on India, the Philippines and Turkey. Only one variable was found to be significant for all three countries and that was the ratio of home-to-foreign price level, a proxy for the equilibrium exchange rate. However, all regression equations had a high first-order serial correlation, ranging between .304 to .987. This, on one hand, suggested that some important variables could have been omitted from the theoretical specification and, on the other, that the reported standard errors were biased downwards.

---

[1] This can be seen by shifting up the supply and demand schedules in Figure 1.

[2] This case has been discussed in detail in the first section of this chapter.

In addition, Culbertson's analysis is not based on a general equilibrium framework. The model also ignores the supply to the black market originating from under-invoicing of exports and smuggling.

Sheikh [1976] focuses on the role of the black market exchange rate as a guide to the policy maker considering exchange rate change. He also deals with the effects of policies like restrictions on current account transactions and tariffs on the black market exchange rate. His analysis shows that the equilibrium in the black foreign exchange market is stable and that under normal conditions, the black market exchange rate lies above the market clearing and the official rates. Since the model is theoretical in nature, the propositions arising out of it have not been empirically verified.

However, this model has some deficiencies in it. It makes use of partial equilibrium demand-supply apparatus and assumes no resale of officially allocated foreign exchange. Furthermore, like Culbertson's model, it ignores the importance of monetary factors in the determination of equilibrium exchange rate in the black market.

Hence, Blejer [1978] built a model in which the monetary factors are the main determinants of the black market exchange rate. Blejer's analysis is based on the usual "monetarist" assumption that a flow monetary disequilibrium can best be measured by the difference between changes in the domestic credit component of the monetary base (which includes variations in the money multiplier), and changes in the domestic demand for real cash balances. He assumes that the domestic rate of inflation is a weighted average of the prices of traded and nontraded goods. While the prices of traded goods are determined exogenously by the world price level through the official exchange rate, the prices of nontradeables respond to a domestic monetary disequilibrium and prices of tradeables. In this way, the domestic rate of inflation is derived as a function of the world inflation rate, changes in the official rate and the rate of domestic monetary disequilibrium.

The black market exchange rate is then determined in Blejer's model by the current flow supplies and demands of foreign exchange. While the former depends on the differential between the black market and the official rate, the latter is a function of the return on holding foreign money. This return, in turn, depends on the expected rate of depreciation of the black market exchange rate and variations in the expected rate of inflation[1]. By equating the flow supply with flow demand, the black market exchange rate is derived as a function of the official exchange rate and the difference between the domestic and foreign inflation rates. By substituting for domestic inflation, the resulting formulation gives changes in the black market exchange rate as a weighted average of the changes in the official exchange rate and the domestic monetary flow disequilibria.

Blejer further assumes that the official exchange rate is administratively determined by the government's reaction function derived from conditions of utility maximization. Whenever the official exchange rate deviates from the relative purchasing-power-parity, the government goes into action to change the official exchange rate, the exact magnitude depending on the reaction function.

A final expression is thus obtained giving changes in the black market exchange rate as a function of world inflation and domestic monetary disequilibria. The model is then tested by Blejer on Brazil, Chile and Columbia. The regression estimates show that the money market flow disequilibria are transmitted to the black market gradually over a two-year period.

However, Blejer's model suffers from many shortcomings. He assumes that the public buys and sells foreign exchange in the black market to alter their portfolio of financial assets and not for the purpose of buying and selling commodities. By doing away with the existence of restrictions on foreign trade, his model does not allow for foreign exchange demanded to pay for goods that are imported without declaration at the border. Thus, all current account needs are implicitly assumed to be satisfied by the official market. Clearly, this is not valid in view of numerous controls on both the current and the capital account transactions, and the restrictions on foreign trade imposed by many developing

[1] This is a proxy variable for variations in domestic and foreign nominal interest rates.

countries, which diverts a part of the demand for foreign exchange from the official to the black market. Besides, since the black market exchange rate is determined by the current flow supplies and demands, Blejer's model lacks a general equilibrium character.

Further, in the equation determining the prices of nontraded goods, Blejer does not attach any coefficient to the prices of tradeables. This suggests that prices of nontraded goods move in the same proportion as the prices of traded goods. This is not realistic for countries where nontraded goods form a substantial proportion of the consumer basket. Moreover, in Blejer's model, the black market exchange rate is positively related with the official rate. That is, whenever the official exchange rate is devalued, the black market exchange rate depreciates. This holds only if the demand for foreign exchange in the black market is independent of the differential between the official and the black market exchange rate. In other words, the foreign exchange in the black market is demanded irrespective of the official exchange rate.

Finally, Fishelson's [1978] paper examines the determinants of the black market exchange rate for Israel. His regression analysis consists of two versions:

In the purchasing-power-parity version, he tests whether changes in inflation rate at home, official exchange rate, expected inflation, expected devaluation and imported price index have a significant effect on the black market exchange rate for the period 1970-1975. He finds that for the inflationary period 1972-1975, the domestic inflation rate and expectations of exchange rate devaluation were the major explanatory variables. But for the period 1970-1972, when the Israeli inflation rate was low, expectations of official devaluation was the primary influence.

The monetary version of his tests relate changes in the black market exchange rate to changes in the quantity of money, in addition to the variables used in the first version. The results indicate that changes in the quantity of money did not have a statistically significant effect on the Israeli black market exchange rate.

5. Conclusions

At the outset of this chapter, I discussed various mechanisms for allocating private goods. Among the nonprice allocation systems, price control with or without rationing was described in detail to show the emergence of a black market in foreign currencies. It was shown that the equilibrium black market exchange rate could lie either above or below the market clearing rate, depending on the penalty structure.

The empirical estimates of under- and over-invoicing on legal trade in India suggested that under-invoicing of exports and imports formed a significant proportion of the official exports and imports, respectively. This indicated that the tariff/subsidy structure in India has been such that incentive is created to under-invoice exports and imports in the presence of controls on foreign exchange trading. Further, the estimates of goods and assets smuggled into India suggested that smuggling as a proportion of official imports is significant.

A critical evaluation of the existing models on the determinants of black markets in foreign currencies pointed to their inadequacies and the restrictiveness of their assumptions. For instance, the models developed by Culbertson and Sheikh were constructed within a partial equilibrium framework with only one source of supply to the black market. Culbertson stressed the resale of officially allocated foreign exchange, while Sheikh emphasized the under-invoicing of exports and smuggling. Blejer assumed that all current account needs were satisfied by the official market and that the black market exchange rate was determined by current flow supplies and demands of foreign exchange.

In the next chapter, I construct a model for the determinants of the black market exchange rate using the "monetarist" assumptions. The model attempts to overcome the weaknesses that I discussed above in the models developed by Sheikh, Culbertson, Blejer and others.

III. The Model

At the outset, I discuss the factors that explain the hoarding of gold and silver in India. In this context, the relationship between smuggling and the black market in foreign exchange is highlighted. In the subsequent sections, I employ static optimization techniques to derive a money demand function for India. It is assumed that money is a kind of a durable consumer or producer good which yields to its holders a flow of services. A similar assumption is made in regard to gold and silver holdings in India. The resulting money demand function is then expressed in terms of its own, and cross prices just like in any demand function in the theory of consumer behaviour.

The domestic price level is derived from the money demand function and is related to the world price level through the official and the black market exchange rates. In addition, the domestic prices of gold and silver are related to their respective world prices to solve for the black market exchange rate. In this way, the black market exchange rate is determined by the interaction of both the goods market and the money market, and by the conditions of stock equilibrium. The relationship between smuggling and the black market for foreign exchange is also incorporated.

I then carry out empirical tests of the resulting model giving the principal determinants of the black market exchange rate using Indian data for a period of nine to ten years. The classical technique of ordinary least squares is employed to estimate the parameters of the model. As the effect of some of the variables is expected to be distributed over a period of time, these variables are lagged using Almon polynomials.

1. Hoarding and the Black Market Exchange Rate

In India the hoarding of gold and silver is widespread[1]. This

[1] "Total gold stocks, accumulated since the second half of the 19th century, were officially estimated to exceed US $ 2.2 bil-

hoarding could be attributed to social and religious customs and to the lack of low-risk alternatives for channelling savings. White and Stanfield [1974, p. 44] have described this phenomenon quite lucidly:
"Hindu tradition says that gold is the noblest of metals, one of the foremost among the things pure and auspicious. When a father sees his new born child, he should touch it with gold; when a person leaves the world, on the burning pyre, a speck of gold should be put in the mouth. Wearing gold brings prosperity and luck, giving it removes one's sins. Gold kills infections, advises a distinguished doctor of Hinduism's traditional Ayurvedic medicine ... In India ... life insurance and old-age insurance are not yet widespread. The traditional insurance is gold."

Besides, gold and silver have served as a readily acceptable collateral for securing credit at relatively low rates of interest. Thus gold and silver could be treated as "financial assets" that are highly liquid but differ from bonds and equities to the extent that they do not give an explicit pecuniary return to their holders in every time period.

The silver stocks that have accumulated in India over the centuries have been sufficient to meet the domestic needs. Due to the exchange controls and the restrictions on the export of silver that have been imposed from time to time, the domestic price of silver has been lower than the price prevailing in the world markets. This has resulted in smuggling of silver out of India, thereby creating one source of supply of foreign exchange in the black market[1]. The picture is somewhat different in the case of gold. The gold needs of India are many times larger than the annual production and official supplies. Because of restrictions on the import of gold into India,

---

lion at the 'old' price of US $ 38 per ounce. Some other estimates were as high as US $ 10 billion. At the December 1975 free market level, India's gold in private hands would have to be estimated at a minimum of US $ 8 to US $ 9 billion" [Pick's Currency Yearbook, 1975-76, p. 701].

[1] "The flow of silver from India has been an important source to world markets for many years. This flow appears to react to price changes, diminishing when prices decline and increasing when they rise" [The Silver Market, 1977, p. 16].

the domestic price of gold has been consistently higher than the world price. This in turn has created an incentive for large-scale smuggling of gold into India, and the demand for foreign exchange for this purpose has fallen onto the black market[1].

The exact relationship of prices of gold and silver with the black market rate in the foreign exchange market will become clear later in this section when a formal expression for the determinants of the black market exchange rate is derived.

2. Money Demand and Utility Maximization

The usual assumption of money being a durable producer and consumer good which yields its holders an unspecified "monetary service" flow, is made. These services, in turn, enter a utility function and the demand for money is then derived from the demand for these unspecified monetary services[2]. The flow of these monetary services derived by an individual can be written as:

$$N = N(M/P) \tag{1}$$

where N is the flow of real monetary services yielded per unit of time, M/P is the stock of real cash balances held. Equation (1) can be viewed as an individual's production

---

[1] "As India's gold needs are many times larger than her annual production of about 3 metric tons, gold smuggling takes place on a very large scale" [Pick's Currency Yearbook, 1975-76, p. 700]. The relationship between gold smuggling and the black market exchange rate is evident from the means used to pay for the smuggled gold. As White and Stanfield write [1974, p. 41], "One means of payment is black market dollars from all over India. The little ships bring them back by the suitcase."

[2] For instance see, Friedman [1956, p. 4]; Patinkin [1965, Ch. 5]; Klein [1974, pp. 931-933].

An "as if" approach is adopted here. It is assumed that money yields utility because it is held.

function for monetary services [Klein, 1974] with M/P assumed to have declining marginal productivity.

Assume that there exists another asset denoted by G (gold) which is held by the individual. This stock of gold yields to its holders a service flow, distinct from that yielded by the stock of money balances[1]. The flow of these services can be written as:

(1a) $O = O(G)$

where G stands for the stock of gold held.

To facilitate comparison with commodities, X is denoted as the flow of commodity services consumed by an individual per unit of time. The individual's utility function can then be written as:

(2) $U = U(X, O, N)$

where X equals the rate of consumption of commodity services, O stands for the consumption of gold services, and N equals the rate of consumption of monetary services.

Now consider the individual's rate of consumption of commodity services. The flow of X that can be purchased and consumed per unit of time by an individual is a function of the rate of net rupee receipts to the individual.

(3) $PxX = (PY + iB)$

where X equals the rate of flow of commodity services; Px is the price of X; Y is the individual's real rate of permanent earnings; B is the rupee value of investments in bonds; i is the rate of return on these financial assets, measured in rupees per unit of time; and P is the general price level. The term in parentheses in (3) is the money income of the individual. As is evident, it is assumed here that no pecuniary return is available on money balances. This assumption

[1] This is evident from the fact that the portfolio of an individual is made up of both gold and money. Also refer to the quotation on page 31.

appears to be quite valid for India.

It is further assumed that the individual has a given total of real nonhuman wealth W defined as follows:

(4) $$W = M/P + B/P + PgG/P$$ [1]

where Pg stands for the price of gold. The individual maximizes his utility subject to his given real human and nonhuman wealth (Y and W). Forming a Lagrangian from (2) and (3),

(5) $$V = U(X, O, N) - L\,[PxX - PY - iB]$$

From (4) above,

(4') $$B = PW - M - PgG$$

Substituting (4') into (5) and differentiating it with respect to the individual's decision variables X, M and G, the necessary conditions for a constrained maximization are:

(6) $$\delta V/\delta X = U_X - L\,(Px) = 0$$

(7) $$\delta V/\delta M = U_N N'\,(1/P) - L\,(i) = 0$$

(8) $$\delta V/\delta G = U_O O' - L\,(iPg) = 0$$

Assuming that second order conditions hold, the optimum quantities of X, G and M are given as follows:

(9) $$L = U_X/Px = U_N N'\,(1/P)/i = U_O O'/iPg$$

Equation (9) states the familiar condition that the marginal

[1] Savings and intertemporal changes in wealth are being assumed away in this model. Therefore, the allocation of wealth to future consumption is not discussed. Further, also implicit in the model is the fact that bonds do not yield any nonpecuniary services. Their role is simply to reflect the capital market clearing interest rate.

utility derived from every good divided by its price must be the same for all goods[1]. The price of services from money is the interest rate and the price of services from gold is the price of gold multiplied by the interest rate[2].

If the analysis for the silver price (Ps) is analogous to that for the gold price and the relevant empirical proxy for Y and W is the permanent income YP, then it follows from the above conditions that the demand for money function can be written as:

$$(10) \qquad (M/P)_d = f(YP, Pms, Pgs, Pss)$$

where subscript d refers to the quantity demanded; Pms stands for the price of services rendered by money; Pgs stands for the price of gold services; Pss stands for the price of silver services; $\delta(M/P)/\delta YP > 0$, $\delta(M/P)/\delta Pms < 0$ and, as long as the substitution effect dominates any income effect, $\delta(M/P)/\delta Pgs > 0$, $\delta(M/P)/\delta Pss > 0$.

From (9), equation (10) can also be written as:

$$(10a) \qquad (M/P)_d = f(i, Pgi/P, Psi/P, YP)$$ [3]

---

[1] In (9) above, L stands for the marginal utility from money income and not for the marginal utility from money as generally believed. The former is defined as the change in an individual's utility from a rupee change in income allocated optimally across all goods and the latter is defined as the change in an individual's utility from a rupee change in his money holdings.

[2] This is to remind the readers that this is a static optimization of the consumer portfolio in the sense that the utility function is defined with reference to a single time period.

[3] The above demand function differs from that found in Boorman [1976], Laidler [1969, Ch. 8] etc., where the opportunity cost of holding money is the rate of return on alternative assets. The demand function in (10) is expressed in terms of own and cross prices of money just like in any demand function in the theory of consumer behaviour. This formulation is similar to the one by Klein [1974].

On the first impression it seems peculiar that in this formulation, I have as arguments both the interest rate and the level of the gold and silver prices. This result stems from the

where i, Pgi, Psi stand for the price of services rendered by money, gold and silver, respectively. Writing (10a) in Cobb-Douglas form,

$$(10b) \qquad (M/P) = i^{-a_1} \cdot (Pgi/P)^{a_2} \cdot (Psi/P)^{a_3} \cdot YP^{a_4}$$

where a_1, a_2, a_3 are, respectively, the price elasticities of money, gold and silver services.

Taking logarithms of (10b),

$$(10c) \qquad \ln M = (1-a_2-a_3)\ln P - (a_1-a_2-a_3)\ln i + a_2 \ln Pg + a_3 \ln Ps + a_4 \ln YP$$

Finally, it is assumed that the money stock in existence adjusts to the quantity demanded reflecting the long-run tendency of the money market to move to the equilibrium. That is,

$$(11) \qquad M_s = M_d$$

where subscript s refers to the quantity supplied.

---

fact that the precious metals are considered to be equivalent to durable asset holdings, yielding a flow of services which is directly related to their cost. This treatment of durables is found in Harberger [1960], Chow [1966, p. 113] and in Jorgenson's studies of postwar investment behaviour [Branson, 1979, p. 231]. The latter ignored the capital gains term in his analysis on the assumption that investors either do not know or do not care what the anticipated capital gains will be when they consider purchasing a capital good. On the other hand, it is worth noting that capital gains are not excluded from the model. They are captured by the permanent income term (YP) which is the relevant empirical proxy for wealth and real permanent earnings.

It is clear that in my formulation, I am assuming that Indian wealth-holders' demand for gold and silver is independent of expectations about future price increases, however formulated.

3. Domestic Price Level

The domestic price level here is assumed to be a weighted average of the prices of traded and nontraded goods. Thus, the domestic price level can be written as follows (in logarithms):

$$\ln P = b \ln Pt + (1-b) \ln Pnt \tag{12}$$

where Pt is the price of traded goods and Pnt is the price of nontraded goods. The term b stands for the share of traded goods in total expenditure. It is hypothesized that India is a small country in the sense that it cannot influence the world prices of tradeables. Because trade takes place at both the official exchange rate (through official channels) and at the black market rate (through smuggling), it is postulated that a weighted average of both of these exchange rates is an appropriate rate to determine the domestic prices of tradeables. Therefore, the expression for prices of tradeables can be written as (again in logarithms):

$$\ln Pt = [c \ln Eo + (1-c) \ln Eb] + \ln Pw \tag{13}$$

where c is the proportion of trade carried through the official channels at the exchange rate Eo defined as the domestic price of foreign currency; Eb is the black market exchange rate defined as the domestic price of foreign currency in the black market; and Pw stands for the world price level.

Further, it should be noted that in a country like India where foreign exchange is allocated at the officially fixed rate, this exchange rate is not relevant for the determination of market prices of traded goods. It only tells us about the rents captured by the government and the importers (and the other users) to whom foreign exchange is made available at the official rate. In terms of equation (13) it suggests that the weight attached to the black market exchange rate Eb should be greater than the share of smuggling in the total trade.

It is further assumed that the prices of nontradeables vary monotonically with the prices of tradeables. An increase in the relative price of traded goods (through a depreciation of Eo or Eb or both or an exogenous change in Pw) creates an excess demand for nontraded goods as the consumers substitute for the traded goods and as the productive resources move into the nontraded sector, causing the prices of nontraded goods to rise. Thus,

$$\text{(14)} \qquad \ln Pnt = e\ (\ln Pt)$$

where e is the elasticity of prices of nontraded goods with respect to the prices of traded goods[1]. By substituting (14) in (12) and then (13) in (12), the following expression is obtained for the domestic price level in India:

$$\text{(15)} \qquad \ln P = [c \ln Eo + (1-c) \ln Eb + \ln Pw]\ z$$

where z stands for [b + (1-b) e].[2]

4. The Black Market Exchange Rate

From (10c) and (11) a solution is obtained for P which is the general price level net of gold and silver prices. This expression is then further substituted in (15)[3] to solve for Eb. Thus,

$$\text{(16)} \qquad \ln Eb = 1/z(1-c)\ [\ln M - a_4 \ln YP + (a_1 - a_2 - a_3) \ln i - a_3 \ln Ps - a_2 \ln Pg - z \ln Pw - zc \ln Eo]$$

But in equation (16), the domestic prices of gold (Pg) and

[1] In the equation dealing with the prices of nontradeables, Blejer does not attach any coefficient to the prices of tradeables, implying that prices of nontradeables move in the same proportion as the prices of tradeables.

[2] If e=1, then z=1, i.e., all goods are traded.

[3] It should be noted that P in (15) is also to be considered net of gold and silver prices. Hence, $(1-a_2-a_3) \ln P$ in the final expression is substituted for [c ln Eo + (1-c) ln Eb + ln Pw] z. The relationship of the domestic prices of gold and silver with world prices is explicitly taken into account in equations (16a) and (16b).

silver (Ps) are related to their respective world prices through the black market exchange rate. Therefore,

$$\ln Pg = \ln Eb + \ln Pg' \quad (16a)$$

$$\ln Ps = \ln Eb + \ln Ps' \quad (16b)$$

where Pg' is the world price of gold, and Ps' is the world price of silver. By substituting (16a) and (16b) in (16), a solution is obtained for Eb. The reduced form obtained is given below.

$$\ln Eb = h_0 - h_1 \ln Eo + h_2 \ln M - h_3 \ln YP + h_4 \ln i - h_5 \ln Ps' - h_6 \ln Pg' - h_7 \ln Pw \quad (17)$$[1]

Equation (17) gives the principal determinants of the exchange rate in the black market for India. They are, respectively, the official exchange rate, the nominal quantity of money, the real level of income, the interest rate, the world prices of gold and silver and the world price level of all goods (excluding the prices of gold and silver)[2]. Thus, the black market exchange rate has been determined in a general equilibrium framework by the interaction of both the goods and the money market. An important feature of this model is that equilibrium prevails in both the flow and the stock markets, so that the black market exchange rate is not determined by the current flow demands and supplies of foreign exchange as in Blejer's model [1978].

---

[1] It is to be noted that the coefficients arrived at in the equation (17) are different from the coefficients of the original structural equations (16), (16a) and (16b).

[2] Since there is no coefficient for the risk involved in transacting in the black market in equation (17), implicitly it is being assumed that the penalty structure does not change during the period to which this model is applied. This is valid for the case of India, where the authorities have more or less tolerated the existence and operation of the unofficial market in foreign currencies, except with the possible exception of one period. There will be more on this in the next section.

At this point, it would be pertinent to emphasize the role of monetary factors in the determination of exchange rate in the black market. The fact that "monetarist" assumptions are made does not mean that the role of "real" factors has been overlooked. In the above model, the "real" factors enter in the form of determinants of demand for real balances, which in turn exert an influence on the exchange rate in the black market. It will be shown below that the equilibrium black market exchange rate can change without any accompanying change in the money supply.

The second term in the equation (the official exchange rate) captures the effect of changes in the official exchange rate on the black market exchange rate. Other things being equal, a higher official exchange rate would reduce the incentive to under-invoice exports, or to over-invoice imports, or increase the incentive to over-invoice exports and divert the flow of remittances by residents abroad from the black market to the official market. Since the demand for foreign exchange in the black market is not independent of the supply of foreign exchange to the official market, increased foreign exchange receipts would lower the demand for foreign exchange in the black market[1].

The next term captures the effect of monetary changes on the black market exchange rate. Other things being equal, a higher monetary growth in India will mean a depreciating exchange rate in the black market.

The fourth term reflects the effect of changes in real income in India on the black market exchange rate. An increase in real income in India through an increased demand for money

---

[1] This is also evident from the partial analysis presented in Chapter II. - In Blejer's model, the black market exchange rate is positively related with the official rate. That is, when the official rate depreciates, contrary to the above results, the black market exchange rate also depreciates. Blejer's result is based on the somewhat unrealistic assumption that the demand for foreign exchange in the black market is independent of the differential between the official and the black market exchange rate. In other words, the foreign exchange will always be demanded in the black market irrespective of the official exchange rate.

would cause the black market exchange rate to appreciate. This term constitutes one of the links between the exchange rate in the black market, monetary sector and the real sector. For instance, it tells us how changes in productivity get reflected in changes in the exchange rate in the black market. The fifth term incorporates the influence of the interest rate in India on the black market exchange rate. A higher interest rate at home through a reduced demand for money will cause the exchange rate in the black market to depreciate.

The next two terms capture the effects of changes in the world prices of gold (Pg') and silver (Ps'). Ceteris paribus, an increase in world price of gold (or silver) would increase the demand for money and cause the black market exchange rate to appreciate [1].

The last term reflects the effect of world prices of all goods (excluding gold and silver) on the exchange rate. The world price level is a function of the money demand and supply conditions in the rest of the world. Other things remaining the same, rising prices in the rest of the world due to monetary expansion in excess of real money demand would cause the black market exchange rate to appreciate [2].

5. Data and Regression Estimates

In this section, the regression estimates of the equation (17) giving the principal determinants of the black market exchange rate in India are presented. The period of estimation ranges from the first quarter of 1967 to the last quarter of

---

[1] The changes in the world prices of gold and silver could also be interpreted to reflect confidence in the dollar. Thus, when gold (and/or silver) appreciate, dollar depreciates and rupee appreciates.

[2] One can substitute money demand and supply conditions in the rest of the world for Pw, as in Dornbusch [1976a], Girton and Roper [1977]] and Sargen [1977]. But to keep this model simple, Connolly and Silveira's (1979] approach of retaining Pw has been adopted.

1975[1]. The dependent variable is expressed as the price of a U. S. dollar in rupees in the black market. The data for the black market exchange rate has been obtained from the Pick's Currency Yearbook[2].

For the variable M (representing money stock in India) in equation (17), M1, consisting of currency, coins and demand deposits has been used. Since quarterly GNP figures for India are not available for the period under study, the real income variable YP has been proxied by the quarterly average of the index of industrial production.

The price of gold in the world market (Pg') refers to the quarterly average of the monthly prices in the London gold market. The quarterly figures for the price of silver in the world market (Ps') are obtained by first approximating the monthly price of silver by averaging the end of the month and the middle of the month prices, and then computing quarterly averages from the monthly figures.

Most of the studies have proxied the world price level (Pw) by the U. S. wholesale price index [Blejer, 1978; Connolly, Silveira, 1979]. As one is really interested in changes in the money supply in excess of real money demand in the U. S., it would be more appropriate to use the U. S. implicit price deflator (which is obtained by dividing the nominal GNP by the real GNP) in place of the U. S. wholesale price index. Thus, the U. S. implicit price deflator has been used as a proxy for the variable Pw. The quarterly average of the call money rate in India has been used as a proxy for the interest variable (i)[3].

During the period under study, variation in the official exchange rate (expressed as price of one U. S. dollar in the

---

[1] Whenever any of the variables in the model are lagged, an equal number of observations of the lagged variable are obtained. This way the 'effective' period covered by this study, 1967-1975, is not shortened.

[2] See Appendix 1 for the definitions of the symbols used in the text and the data sources.

[3] The other available proxy is the yield on government bonds. But the change in it between 1967-1975 is barely noticeable.

official market) was relatively insignificant[1]. Therefore, this variable has been incorporated in the intercept term.

Since the effect of the variables M, YP and Pw on the dependent variable is distributed over a period of time, these variables have been lagged up to four quarters. For this purpose, Almon polynomials of second degree constrained on the right have been used[2].

Table 6 presents the regression estimates of the equation (17). The adjusted R^2 is relatively high and the regression equation is significant at the 1 per cent level. The D. W. statistic is 2, suggesting absence of first-order serial correlation. The latter also suggests that no important variable has been omitted from the theoretical specification.

Table 6 - Regression Estimates of Equation (17), 1967-1975

Variable (ln)	Coefficient	t-value	Statistics	
Constant	3.893	9.93**	R^2	0.894
Ps'	-0.004	-0.05	Adjusted R^2	0.827
Pg'	-0.519	-5.47**	F-statistic	24.233
i	0.065	1.92*	SER	0.045
M	0.821	3.03**	D. W. statistic	2.022
YP	-0.850	-2.73**		
Pw	0.259	0.55		

** = Significant at the 5 per cent level; * = significant at the 10 per cent level. - Two-tailed test.

[1] For instance, the official exchange rate (expressed in terms of a U. S. dollar) stood at around Rs 7.5 from 1967 to 1973. It rose slightly to around Rs 8 during 1974-1975.

[2] An unconstrained lag structure (which is not reported here) was also tried. The results presented in Table 6 are not very different from them. The notable difference was a higher D. W. statistic (2.29), with approximately the same F statistic.

All the variables have the right signs except the world price level variable (Pw). But the latter is not significantly different from zero. The coefficients attached to the variables Pg', YP and M enter the regression at the 5 per cent level of significance and the variable (i) enters the regression at the 10 per cent level of significance. The variable Ps' has the right sign but is statistically insignificant. This could be attributed to the fact that from time to time Indian government has permitted the official exports of silver by way of export quotas etc., with part of the receipts entering the official reserves.

Table 7 reports the estimates of each of the distributed lags for M, YP and Pw, respectively. (In Table 6, only the sums of the lagged coefficients are presented.) The coefficients

Table 7 - Estimated Lag Distribution of Money Supply (M), Income (YP) and World Price Level (Pw)

Variable	Coefficient	t-value
M(t-0)	-0.359	-0.84
M(t-1)	0.246	3.03**
M(t-2)	0.508	1.92*
M(t-3)	0.426	1.71
Pw(t-0)	1.717	3.35**
Pw(t-1)	0.078	0.55
Pw(t-2)	-0.754	-2.31**
Pw(t-3)	-0.780	-2.60**
YP(t-0)	-1.253	-3.44**
YP(t-1)	-0.255	-2.73**
YP(t-2)	0.286	1.60
YP(t-3)	0.371	2.17**

** = Significant at the 5 per cent level; * = significant at the 10 per cent level. - Two-tailed test.

of the money supply variable referring to the quarters t-i for i = 1, 2 are significantly different from zero and the coefficient of quarter t-0 is not significantly different from zero. It seems therefore that the effect of monetary expansion on the black market exchange rate begins in the second quarter.

The coefficients of Pw referring to quarters t-i for i > 2 have the expected sign and are significant at the 5 per cent level. But the coefficient of the first quarter has the wrong sign and is significantly different from zero. This suggests that the black market exchange rate overshoots the long-run equilibrium level when the world price level rises.

In the equation (17), it was implicitly assumed that the penalty structure remains unchanged during the period to which this model is applied. There is, however, some period covered by this study during which the probability of conviction could have altered. To test if the emergency imposed by Mrs. Gandhi in June/July 1975 and the crackdown on people operating in this market prior to it had any significant effect on the black market exchange rate, a dummy variable was tried for the last four and five quarters. The results (not reported here) showed, however, that none of these factors had any statistically significant effect on the black market exchange rate.

6. Conclusions

In this chapter, I developed a model for the determinants of the black market in foreign exchange for India. This model attempted to improve upon the models built by authors like Culbertson and Blejer. This was achieved by

(1) allowing for interaction between smuggling and the black market for foreign currencies and

(2) determining the black market exchange rate in a general equilibrium framework, by using the conditions of stock equilibrium in which a flow equilibrium is implicit.

The reduced form expression obtained showed that the principal determinants of the exchange rate in the black market in India are the official exchange rate, the nominal quantity of money, the real level of income and the interest rate, the world prices of gold and silver, and the world price level.

The regression results of the reduced form were generally supportive of the formulation. The world price of gold, the real income, the domestic money supply and the interest rate were found to have a statistically significant effect on the black market exchange rate. The results also suggest that the effects of a monetary expansion at home, and of a change in the world price level on the dependent variable begin to show in the second and third quarters, respectively. Furthermore, it was found that the black market exchange rate overshoots the long-run equilibrium level when the world price changes.

IV. On the Efficiency of Black Markets in Foreign Currencies

There is an overwhelming empirical literature in support of the proposition that the stock market is efficient in the sense that prices fully reflect all the publicly available information[1]. In an efficient market, traders collect and process all the information available to them in order to assess the value of an asset. Thus, the market prices at which trade takes place continuously reflects this information, thereby eliminating any extra-normal profit opportunities.

Since some of the major currencies have been floating over the last seven years, interest has been directed to the question of efficiency of foreign exchange markets in processing the available information[2]. Most of the empirical work generally supports the hypothesis that the foreign exchange markets are efficient in the weak-form sense[3]. In some countries trading in foreign currencies takes place in black markets. The reasons for the emergence of these markets were discussed in some detail in the earlier chapters. The discussion focused on the various restrictions that are placed on the foreign sector. The importance of these markets in sustaining illegal import and export of goods and assets, as well as illegal capital flows has been growing in the past few years[4]. The relevant question to be analysed in this chapter

---

[1] See, for instance, Fama et al. [1969] and Fama [1970].

[2] See, for instance, Giddy, Dufey [1975], Burt et al. [1977], Levich [1978], Cornell, Dietrich [1978], Logue et al. [1978].

[3] In the literature, there exist three versions of the efficient market hypothesis. The first, the so-called weak form asserts that successive changes in prices are independent of the sequence of past prices. That is, the historical record of prices contains no information which can be used by market participants to forecast future prices. The semi-strong form deals with the speed of price adjustment to other "obviously publicly available information" [Fama, 1970]. Finally, the strong form says that not only public information but all information is fully reflected in prices.

[4] For some empirical estimates of over- and under-invoicing of exports, imports and smuggling in India, see Chapter II.

is whether these markets are weak-form efficient. One implication of efficiency would be that black market exchange rates are good indicators of market trends. Another one would be that changes in the official exchange rate could be "forecasted" by changes in the black market rate.

In the black markets for foreign currencies the information about prices and market participants is generally imperfect, making price comparisons difficult. Further, these markets tend to be thin and often segmented. Moreover, the transaction costs, as measured by the buy-sell differential, could also be high. These factors could hinder efficient adjustment of exchange rates to new information[1].

In the following section, I discuss various models of the weak-form version of the efficient market hypothesis with reference to exchange rates. The most appropriate model is then used to carry out the market efficiency tests on black markets in foreign currencies. These tests are based on the autocorrelation functions of rates of return on currency positions, on nonparametric tests like the runs analysis, and on the mechnical trading rules applied to historical currency prices in the black market. The overall results suggest that the hypothesis that black market are efficient at least in the weak form cannot be rejected. Hence, the cross-correlations between the changes in the black market rate and changes in the official exchange rate are examined to see if the black market exchange rate "predicts" the movements in the official rate.

1. The Efficient Market Hypothesis: Alternative Models

In this section, no distinction is made between freely floating exchange rates and the black market exchange rates. The term "exchange rate" refers to both[2].

---

[1] It is worth noting that these conditions are not necessary for the efficient adjustment of prices. For a detailed explanation see Fama [1970].

[2] This section relies heavily on Giddy and Dufey [1975] and Granger and Morgenstern [1970].

The strong-form version of the efficient market hypothesis which asserts that exchange rates "fully reflect" all the publicly available information is too general to be tested empirically. To make this hypothesis testable, the process of price formation needs to be specified in greater detail. This can be achieved by assuming that the condition of market equilibrium can be stated in terms of expected returns. Notationally, it can be described as follows:

$$(18) \qquad E(\tilde{X}_{t+1} \mid \phi_t) = [1 + E(\tilde{R}_{t+1} \mid \phi_t)]\ X_t$$

where E is the expected value operator; X_t is the exchange rate at time t; R_t is the one-period rate of return; ϕ_t represents that set of information which is assumed to be fully reflected in the exchange rate at t.

The process that determines the exchange rate can be described as follows. At time t, the market uses the given information set ϕ_t to assess the probability distribution of $\tilde{X}_{t+1}$. The mean of this distribution is the expected future exchange rate, $E(\tilde{X}_{t+1} \mid \phi_t)$. This assessment of the distribution of $\tilde{X}_{t+1}$ coupled with some model of equilibrium expected return then determines $E(\tilde{R}_{t+1} \mid \phi_t)$. The $E(\tilde{R}_{t+1} \mid \phi_t)$ in conjunction with $E(\tilde{X}_{t+1} \mid \phi_t)$ determines the equilibrium exchange rate at t, X_t. It is in this sense that the information set ϕ_t is fully reflected in the formation of X_t.

From the process of exchange rate determination described above, a test of market efficiency is a simultaneous test of efficiency and of the assumptions of market equilibrium. If the null hypothesis (that the market is efficient) cannot be rejected, then this implies that the assumptions about market equilibrium cannot be rejected either. Conversely, if the null hypothesis is rejected, then the problem lies in deciding whether to reject the hypothesis of market efficiency or the assumptions of the underlying market model. The results show that in fact markets are efficient so that the above problem did not have to be resolved.

The information set needed to carry out strong-form tests is not generally available to researchers studying events ex post. Therefore, the concept of market efficiency has been discussed with reference to the information set consisting of only the series of past prices and returns. This is the weak-form version of the efficient market hypothesis. The variants of this version of the efficient market hypothesis are discussed below.

Hypothesis 1 (Martingale)

When all new information that can potentially affect exchange rates is reflected in the actions of the participants in the foreign exchange market, the exchange rate has an equal probability of appreciating or depreciating. Therefore, the exchange rate expected to prevail in the next time period, irrespective of the information available to the forecaster, is simply the present exchange rate. The exchange rate series is then said to follow a martingale:

$$E(\tilde{X}_{t+1}) = E(\tilde{X}_{t+1} \mid \phi'_t)$$

$$= E(\tilde{X}_{t+1} \mid \phi_t)$$

(19) $$= X_t$$

ϕ_t denotes all the publicly available information at time t; ϕ'_t represents the series of present and past values of X_t, i. e., X_t, X_{t-1} ..., ϕ'_t is a subset of ϕ_t, i. e., ϕ'_t contains at most the information in ϕ_t but it could not contain more[1].

Or, equivalently, let:

$$R_t = \ln X_t - \ln X_{t-1} \approx (X_t - X_{t-1}) / X_{t-1}$$

---

[1] When $\tilde{X}_t$ is a martingale, then the same holds for $\ln \tilde{X}_t$. For details, see Giddy and Dufey [1975, p. 8].

R_t is the rate of change of the exchange rate, or the return from holding the foreign currency from t-1 to t. [1]

$$E(\tilde{R}_{t+1}) = E(\tilde{R}_{t+1} \mid \phi'_t)$$

$$= E(\tilde{R}_{t+1} \mid \phi_t)$$

$$= 0 \quad (20)$$

That is, the expected return on holding foreign currency with respect to the information sequence (ϕ_t) is zero. In other words, sequence ($\tilde{R}_t$) is a "fair game" with respect to the information sequence (ϕ_t). Thus, given that the exchange rate follows a martingale, the E ($\tilde{R}_{t+1}$) is a constant. When $\tilde{R}_t$ is further restricted to being serially independent and identically distributed, then the above model becomes a random walk[2].

$$\tilde{R}_t = \ln X_t - \ln X_{t-1}$$

$$\ln \tilde{X}_t = \ln \tilde{X}_{t-1} + \tilde{R}_t \quad (21)$$

where $E(\tilde{R}_t) = 0$, $Cov(\tilde{R}_t, \tilde{R}_{t-j}) = 0$, for all $j \neq 0$. However, it is not necessary for the purposes of testing the efficient

[1] There are two main reasons for using the logarithmic form. First, it facilitates the comparison between yields on holding foreign currencies and securities, especially when for changes less than $\pm$ 15 per cent the change in log price approximates the percentage price change. (For a proof of this statement, see Fama [1965, p. 45].) Second, it eliminates the effect of scale. That is, it overcomes the possible problems which could arise with observations that are widely different in magnitude.

[2] For a brief history of the random walk model and the specific names that have been given to this model, see Granger and Morgenstern [1970, Ch. 3].

market hypothesis to impose the aforementioned restrictions on $\tilde{R}_t$. All that is required is that $\tilde{R}_t$ have a finite variance. It is worth noting that a pair of variables can be serially uncorrelated yet not be independent[1]. Therefore, the following discussion and tests revolve around a martingale rather than a random walk model in the strict sense.

It follows from (19) and (20) that today's exchange rate is the best predictor of any future exchange rates and that the sequence $\tilde{R}_t$ is a fair game.

From (21),

$$\ln \tilde{X}_{t+1} = \ln \tilde{X}_t + \tilde{R}_{t+1}$$

By successive substitution, the following result is obtained:

$$\ln \tilde{X}_{t+n} = \ln \tilde{X}_t + \sum_{j=1}^{n} \tilde{R}_{t+j}$$

$$E\,(\ln \tilde{X}_{t+n}) = \ln X_t + \sum_{j=1}^{n} E\,(\tilde{R}_{t+j})$$

(because $\tilde{R}_t$ is uncorrelated, $E\,(R_{t+j}) = 0$, all j)

$$(22) \qquad = \ln X_t$$

That is, the best predictor of any future exchange rate is the present exchange rate.

---

[1] Only when two random variables come from a bivariate normal distribution and have a zero correlation can one conclude that these variables are independent. For a detailed discussion on this, see Granger and Morgenstern [1970, Ch. 3].

Further, define

$$\tilde{R}'_{t+n} = \ln \tilde{X}_{t+n} - \ln \tilde{X}_t$$

then

$$E\,(\tilde{R}'_{t+n}) = E \ln (\tilde{X}_{t+n}) - \ln X_t$$

Using (22) from above,

$$= \ln X_t - \ln X_t$$

(23) $$= 0$$

That is, the expected return on holding a foreign currency for any period is zero.

One major implication of (22) and (23) is, that any forecast based on past values of exchange rates will do no better than the simple martingale model.

Hypothesis 2 (Submartingale)

The hypothesis 1 implicitly assumed that traders hold foreign exchange in non-interest bearing forms like specie or demand deposits and that there are no lending and borrowing opportunities. Clearly, this is not always the case. The submartingale form of the efficient market hypothesis corrects for this deficiency. According to this version, the best forecast of the future exchange rate is the present exchange rate after it has been adjusted for the differences in returns that can be earned in each of the two currencies. Thus, not only does the new information influence the behaviour of the traders, but the latter also take into account the interest earnings and losses (whichever is the case) on holdings of foreign currency. The exchange rate series (X_t) follows a submartingale with respect to any information sequence (ϕ_t):

$$E(\tilde{X}_{t+1} \mid i_D, i_F) = E(\tilde{X}_{t+1} \mid i_D, i_F, \phi_t')$$

$$= E(\tilde{X}_{t+1} \mid i_F, i_D, \phi_t)$$

(24) $$= X_t f(i_D, i_F) \gtreqless X_t$$

where i_D and i_F stand for the yields on domestic and foreign interest bearing instruments, respectively. The submartingale form can also be expressed in terms of the rates of return [1]

(25) $$E(\tilde{R}_{t+1} \mid i_D, i_F) \gtreqless 0$$

From the above discussion, it appears that a submartingale is theoretically an appropriate model for testing market efficiency in the weak-form sense. It is implicitly being assumed that the underlying determinants of the exchange rate in the black market are generated by a stationary stochastic process. This enables one to apply the martingale or submartingale models to the exchange rate sequence (X_t).

2. A Brief Overview of the Existing Studies

Recently, two papers have specifically tested for the efficiency of the black markets in foreign currencies. In the first study, Fishelson [1978] analysed the speed of adjustment of exchange rates in the black market to new information, which is the semi-strong version of the efficient market hypothesis. He examined whether changes in spot rates of the British pound, the German mark and the Swiss franc in the European exchange markets are transmitted to the Israeli black market. This analysis is based on the assumption that the black

---

[1] For derivation of (24) and (25), see Giddy and Dufey [1975, pp. 12-14].

market predominantly exists for the leading currency, the U. S. dollar. Given the price of the U. S. dollar in the black market (in terms of Israeli pounds), the exchange rates in the black market for the above currencies can be estimated by taking the product of the price of the U. S. dollar in the black market and the European spot rates (expressed in terms of the U. S. dollar). The coefficients of his regression analysis were generally supportive of perfect arbitrage in the black markets. For instance, a one per cent increase in the price of the British pound in terms of the U. S. dollar raises the price of the British pound in terms of the Israeli pound by one per cent. However, there was one problem. The results contained significant first-order serial correlation. This suggested that there is some lag before information is fully transmitted to the Israeli exchange market. This was explained by Fishelson in terms of (a) caution on the part of the traders and (b) lack of a forward market in black foreign exchange.

In the other study, Giddy [1978b] examined weekly changes in the black market premium for Brazil, Peru and Israel. By identifying and fitting ARIMA models[1] to the sequence of the first differences of black market premia, he concluded that the black market for all three countries is efficient in the weak-form sense.

3. Data

The empirical tests presented in this chapter have been carried out on both the monthly and the weekly black market exchange rates for India, South Korea and Taiwan. The black market exchange rate (Xb_t) is defined as the price of one U. S. dollar in domestic currency in the black market. The monthly observations of the black market exchange rate refer to the end-of-month price of the U. S. dollar and have been collected

[1] ARIMA (Autoregressive Integrated Moving Average) models are fitted on the exchange rate series by the use of Box and Jenkins [1976] techniques. The essential idea is to model the series so that the residuals are reduced to white noise. For a simplified discussion on ARIMA models, see Nelson [1973].

Figure 4 - Plot of Black Market Exchange Rate and of Rates of Return on Weekly Positions for the Indian Rupee

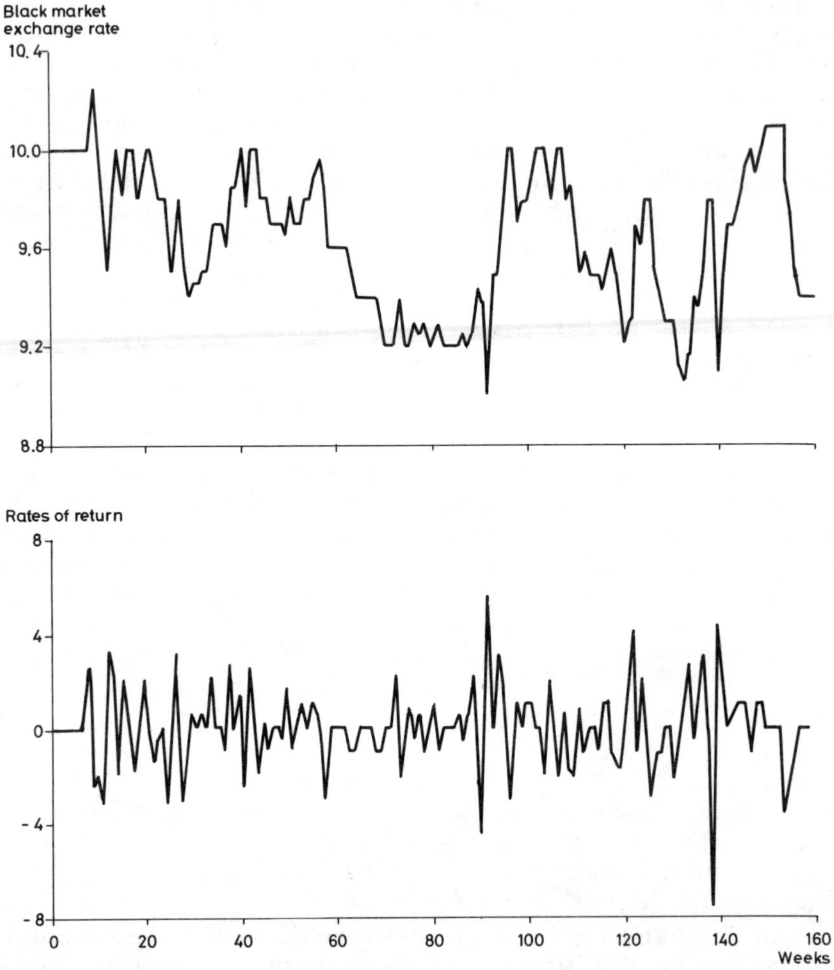

Figure 5 - Plot of Black Market Exchange Rate and of Rates of Return on Monthly Positions for the Indian Rupee

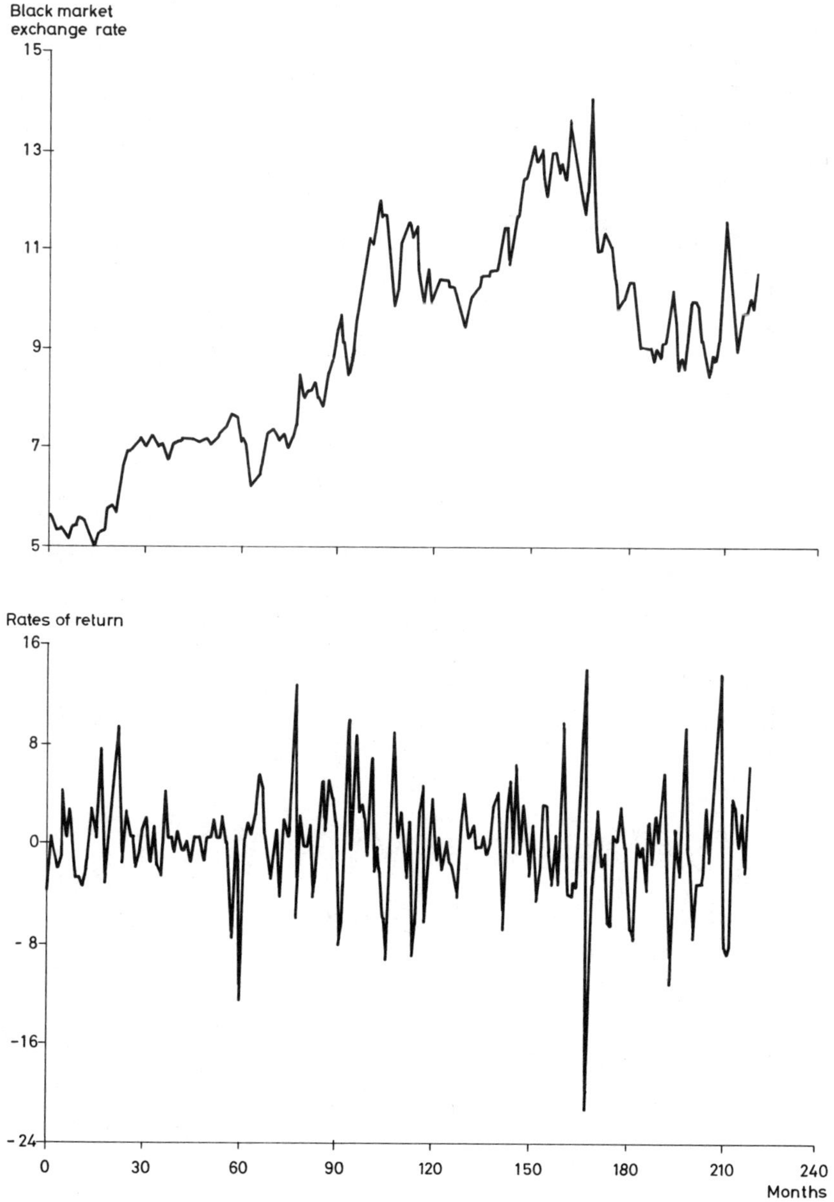

Figure 6 - Plot of Black Market Exchange Rate and of Rates of Return on Weekly Positions for the South Korean Won

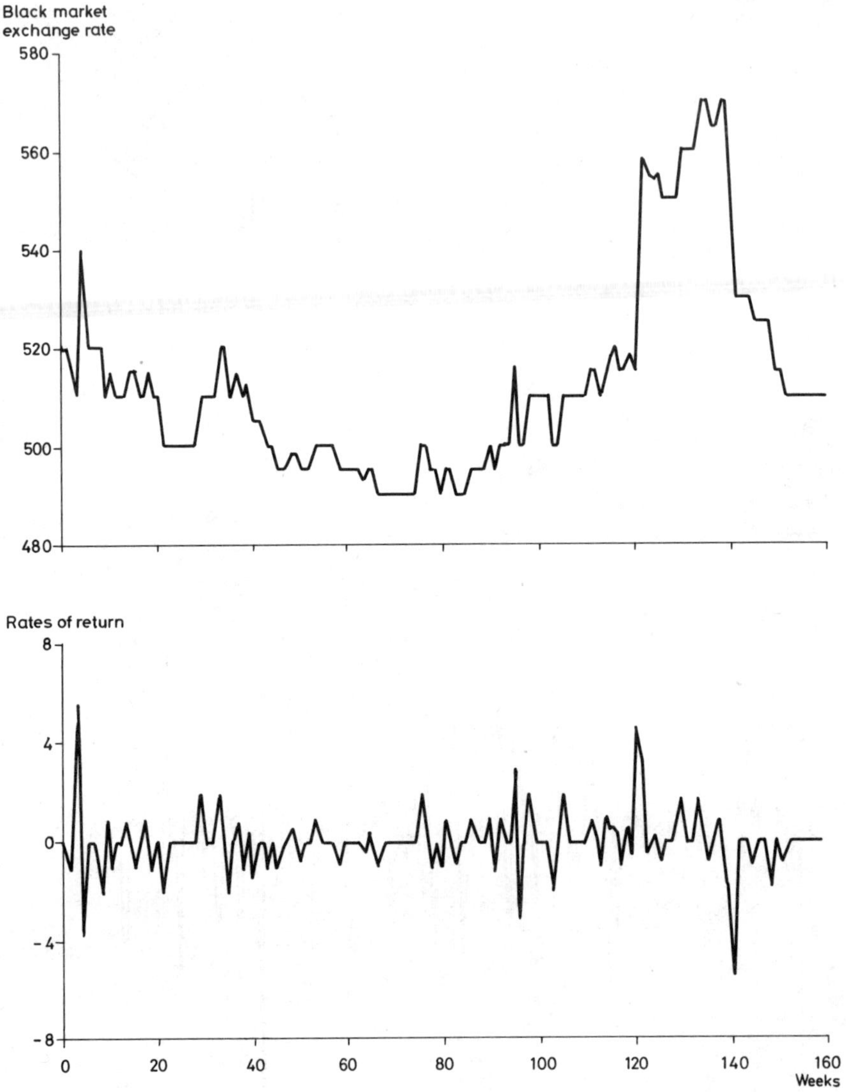

Figure 7 - Plot of Black Market Exchange Rate and of Rates of Return on Monthly Positions for the South Korean Won

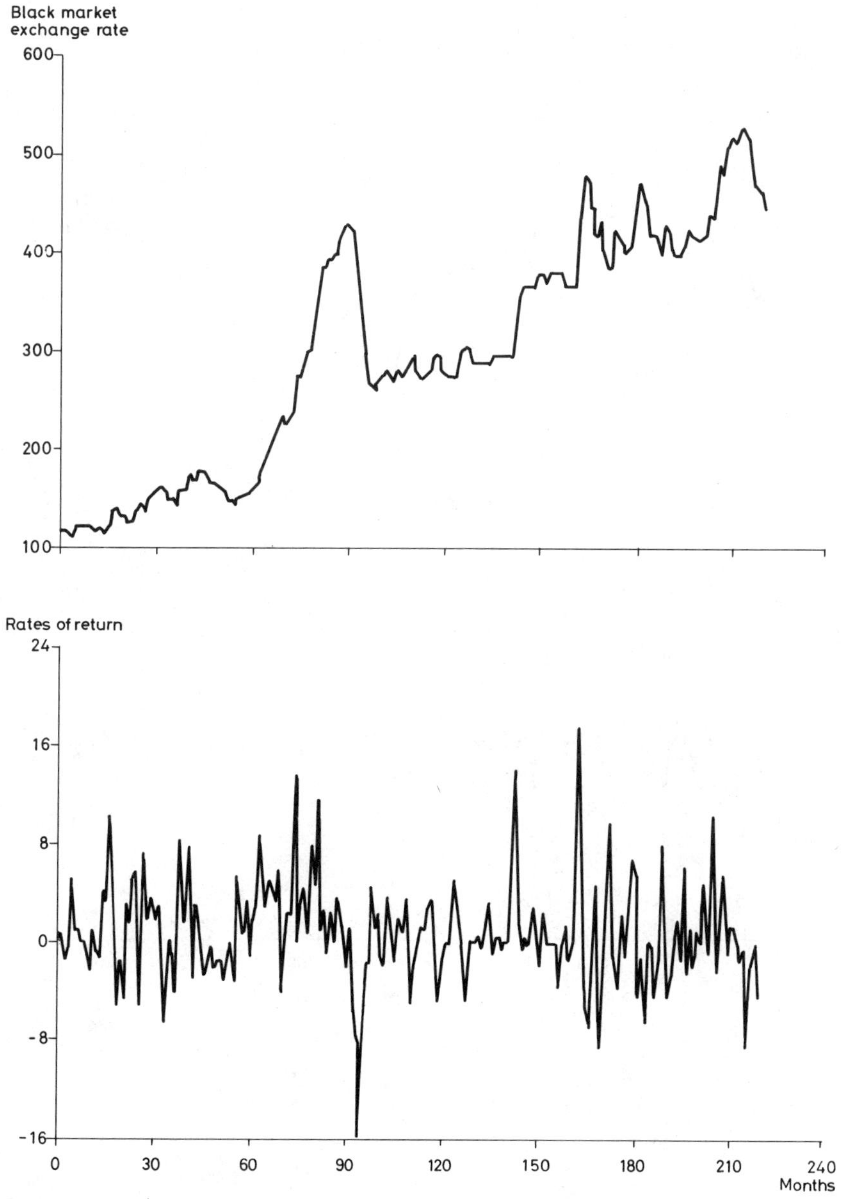

Figure 8 - Plot of Black Market Exchange Rate and of Rates of Return on Weekly Positions for the Taiwan Dollar

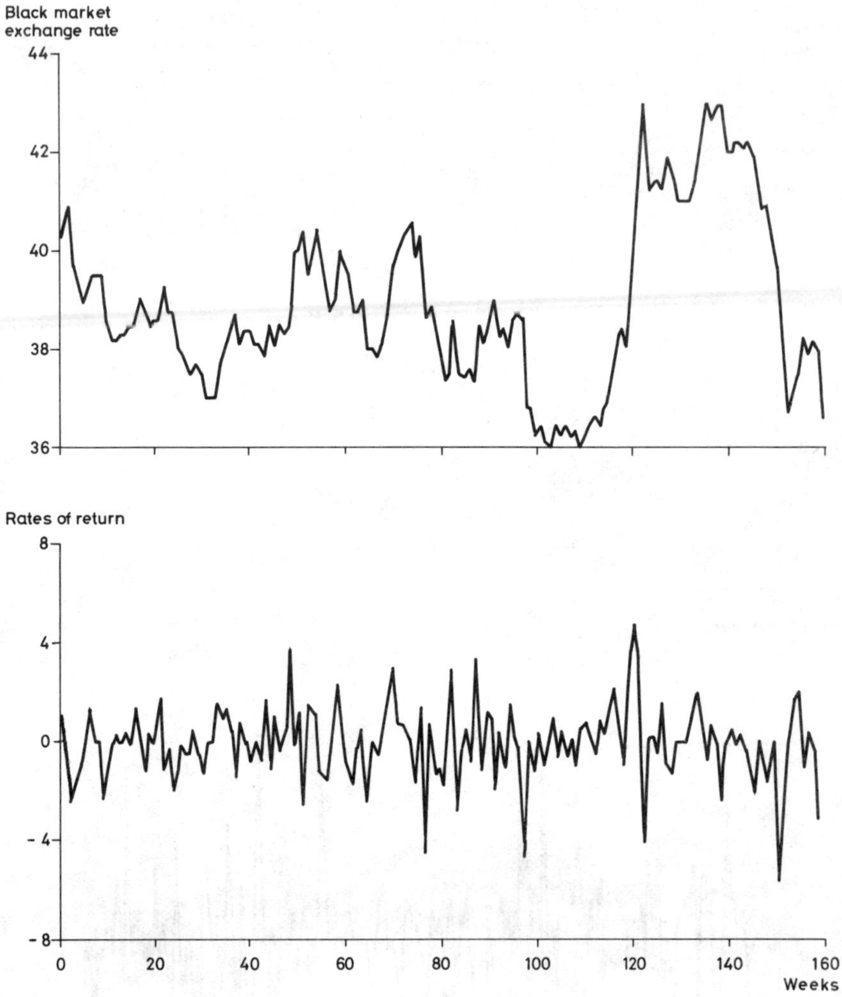

Figure 9 - Plot of Black Market Exchange Rate and of Rates of Return on Monthly Positions for the Taiwan Dollar

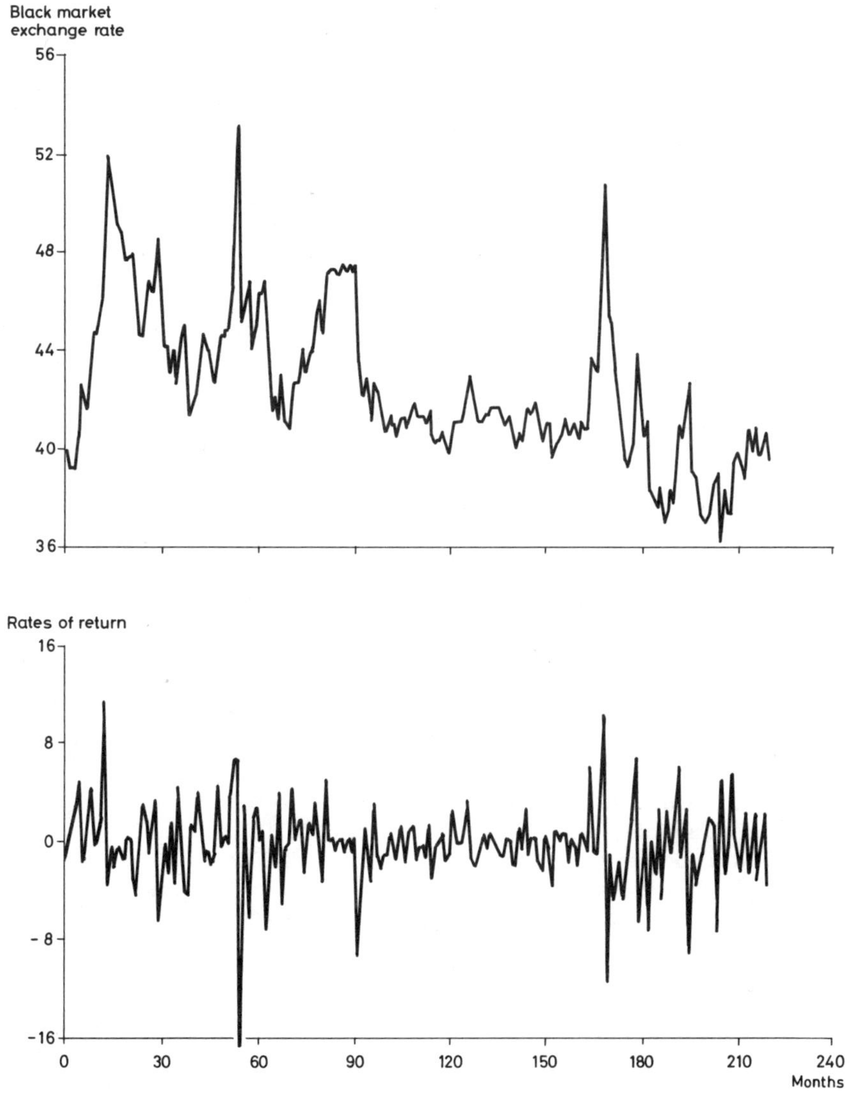

from the Pick's Currency Yearbook[1]. These rates are for transactions that take place physically within the country and at some of the major trading centres of the world. The monthly period ranges from January 1958 to March 1976[2]. The official exchange rate (Xo_t) is defined as the price of a U. S. dollar in the official market in terms of domestic currency. The data for these monthly series for the same period has been obtained from the International Financial Statistics[3].

The weekly black market exchange rate used in this study is the selling price of the U. S. dollar prevailing on Tuesdays[4]. The data for these exchange rate series and the weekly official rate series has been collected from the Far Eastern Economic Review, a Hongkong-based weekly. The weekly period consists of 159 weeks, starting on September 7, 1976 and ending on September 18, 1979[5].

The statistical tests for efficiency are performed on the first differences of natural logarithms of the exchange rate series. These tests consist of the statistical significance of autocorrelation functions, the analysis of runs and the Alexanderian filter rules.

---

1 These rates are supplied by the foreign correspondents of "Pick's World Currency Report" and currency dealers in the various trading centres.

2 In June of 1962, the South Korean hwan was abolished and replaced by the won, which was set equal to 10 hwans. The data from January 1958 to May 1962 has therefore been adjusted accordingly. Since no observation is available for June 1962, the previous month's value has been used in its place.

3 For India and Taiwan, the official exchange is the selling price for one U. S. dollar at the end of month up to December 1974 and March 1975, respectively, and thereafter it is the midpoint rate. For South Korea, it is the principal official rate up to December 1974 and thereafter the central bank rate.

4 However, there are a few exceptions. Six observations refer to the exchange rate on Mondays and two to the rate prevailing on the previous Tuesday.

5 The period of study for both the weekly and the monthly series has been determined by the availability of data.

The plots of each of the exchange rate series and of the first differences of their natural logarithms are presented in Figures 4 through 9. Because of the opportunity cost of holding foreign exchange, the first differences ought to be adjusted for relative interest rates. The theoretical justification for this adjustment was discussed in detail in the previous section. But, given the difficulty of finding interest yielding assets that are of comparable risk for the countries in question, such adjustments were not carried out.

4. Empirical Results

The Autocorrelation Functions

Sample autocorrelations of the first differences of the natural logarithms of both the monthly and weekly exchange rate series were computed. The Tables 8 through 10 report the coefficients of the autocorrelation functions for up to 24 lags. The results show that three coefficients are significant for the weekly series and three for the monthly series. In the latter case, all the significant coefficients are observed in the South Korean series whereas, in the former case, two coefficients are significant for the Indian rupee and only one for the Taiwan dollar. However, one should not be overly concerned with these indications of dependence in the series of rates of return[1]. The few significant autocorrelation coefficients could simply be due to sampling errors. Moreover, the observed distributions of rates of return were leptokurtic [2]. The significance of such a distribution is that the probability of large or small changes is greater than would be expected under a normal distribution. Hence, tests of statistical significance based on the assumption of a normal distribution could mislead the researcher into thinking that there is de-

---

[1] For a random data set, one would expect one coefficient to be significant for every twenty calculated. Hence, for India, the number of significant coefficients is slightly higher than expected if the series were random.

[2] The same has been observed in the studies dealing with stock markets [Fama, 1965] and freely floating exchange rates [Giddy, Dufey, 1975; Burt et al., 1977; Cornell, Dietrich, 1978].

Table 8 - Autocorrelation Functions of Weekly and Monthly Series for India

Lag	Coefficient	Lag	Coefficient	Lag	Coefficient
		159 weeks[a]			
1	-0.12	9	-0.18*	17	-0.09
2	-0.18*	10	-0.09	18	-0.07
3	0.06	11	0.09	19	0.11
4	0.00	12	-0.02	20	-0.08
5	-0.08	13	0.11	21	0.01
6	0.02	14	-0.12	22	0.01
7	0.08	15	-0.15	23	0.02
8	0.08	16	0.16	24	-0.01
		219 months[b]			
1	0.09	9	0.13	17	0.00
2	-0.09	10	0.02	18	-0.01
3	-0.13	11	0.11	19	0.00
4	-0.12	12	0.08	20	0.03
5	-0.05	13	0.01	21	0.00
6	-0.03	14	-0.03	22	0.06
7	0.07	15	-0.13	23	0.02
8	-0.05	16	-0.05	24	-0.05

[a] September 7, 1976 to September 18, 1979. - [b] January 1958 to March 1976. - *Significant at the 5 per cent level.

Table 9 - Autocorrelation Functions of Weekly and Monthly Series for South Korea

Lag	Coefficient	Lag	Coefficient	Lag	Coefficient
		159 weeks[a]			
1	-0.11	9	0.00	17	-0.03
2	-0.10	10	0.09	18	-0.09
3	0.04	11	-0.03	19	-0.05
4	0.06	12	-0.04	20	-0.14
5	-0.02	13	0.03	21	0.00
6	0.02	14	0.06	22	-0.02
7	-0.03	15	-0.09	23	0.09
8	0.04	16	0.15	24	0.05
		219 months[b]			
1	0.27*	9	0.02	17	0.06
2	0.12	10	0.08	18	-0.01
3	0.05	11	-0.11	19	-0.01
4	-0.04	12	-0.03	20	0.03
5	0.02	13	0.00	21	-0.17*
6	0.01	14	-0.18*	22	-0.11
7	0.01	15	-0.07	23	-0.05
8	0.04	16	0.04	24	-0.08

[a]September 7, 1976 to September 18, 1979. - [b]January 1958 to March 1976. - *Significant at the 5 per cent level.

Table 10 - Autocorrelation Functions of Weekly and Monthly Series for Taiwan

Lag	Coefficient	Lag	Coefficient	Lag	Coefficient
		159 weeks[a]			
1	0.02	9	-0.06	17	0.04
2	0.05	10	0.09	18	-0.13
3	-0.07	11	-0.11	19	-0.01
4	-0.04	12	0.02	20	0.11
5	0.17*	13	0.08	21	0.08
6	-0.08	14	0.01	22	-0.03
7	0.03	15	0.04	23	0.01
8	-0.09	16	-0.05	24	-0.10
		219 months[b]			
1	-0.13	9	0.01	17	0.06
2	-0.10	10	-0.08	18	-0.10
3	0.06	11	0.01	19	-0.09
4	-0.05	12	0.01	20	0.01
5	-0.02	13	0.00	21	-0.03
6	-0.06	14	-0.05	22	-0.06
7	-0.06	15	-0.04	23	0.04
8	0.10	16	-0.02	24	0.11

[a]September 7, 1976 to September 18, 1979. - [b]January 1958 to March 1976. - *Significant at the 5 per cent level.

pendency when in fact there is none. Since the number of significant coefficients was very small, the results reported in Tables 8 through 10 were considered to support the weak-form version of the efficient market hypothesis.

The Box-Pierce statistic is used to test the significance of the autocorrelation functions[1]. Under the null hypothesis of zero autocorrelations,

$$Q = N \sum_{j=1}^{24} \hat{\rho}_j^2 \tag{26}$$

where

N = the number of observations and

$\hat{\rho}_j$ = the estimated autocorrelation at lag j

will be approximately χ^2 distributed with j degrees of freedom. The estimated values of Q reported in Table 11 were compared with the tabulated value of χ^2 for 24 degrees of freedom and the 5 per cent level of significance. The estimated values of the Q-statistic for all but the South Korean monthly series were below the critical value of χ^2. This implies that the weekly rates of return on all the three currencies and monthly rates of return on the Indian rupee and the Taiwan dollar are uncorrelated over the time period studied. These results based on the autocorrelation functions are consistent not only with the hypothesis that the black foreign exchange markets for these currencies are efficient, but also with the assumptions underlying the market equilibrium model.

---

[1] The Box-Pierce statistic has been devised to test the significance of correlation between observations in a given series. This statistic is used here to determine how strong the correlation is between rates of return on currency positions. The Q-statistic has a χ^2 distribution. If the calculated value of Q from the exchange rate series falls below the critical value obtained from the χ^2 distribution table, the correlation between the rates of return is considered to be statistically insignificant.

Table 11 - The Q-Test on Weekly and Monthly Series

Currency	Q-Statistic	
	weekly series	monthly series
Indian rupee	35.676	26.596
South Korean won	18.707	45.845*
Taiwan dollar	21.58	22.192

*Significant at the 5 per cent level.

Indications of dependency in the South Korean won series could be explained by shifts in the mean of the process from one period to another (i.e., the process generating the first differences of the natural logarithms of the exchange rate series may be mean nonstationary) [1]. Under these conditions, the measured autocorrelations may misrepresent the true evolution of the series [2].

The following Figure shows how shifts in the mean of a stochastic process could bias autocorrelation tests in favour of market inefficiency. Suppose the mean of the stochastic process a' in the first sub-period unexpectedly shifts to a'' in the second half of the period. If this shift is unanticipated, it cannot profitably be exploited and is therefore consistent with market efficiency. If the rates of return on the currency positions are uncorrelated in each of the sub-periods, the regression lines for the first and second sub-periods will tend to be horizontal through a' and a'', respectively. But when

[1] For a discussion of stationarity and nonstationarity, see Nelson [1973, Ch. 2].

[2] Sweeney [1978], while studying the efficiency of the goods market, examined the autocorrelation structure of the inflation rate series for some western countries. He found a number of significant autocorrelation coefficients. However, when he segmented the series, the number of significant coefficients were not greater than expected with a random series. This was indicative of mean nonstationarity. Further, when he incorporated the nonstationarity of the process in his hypothesis, any evidence of inefficiency was rejected.

the data for the entire period is pooled, the regression line will tend to be biased towards the 45-degree line and the autocorrelation coefficients for lags one and beyond could appear to be significant.

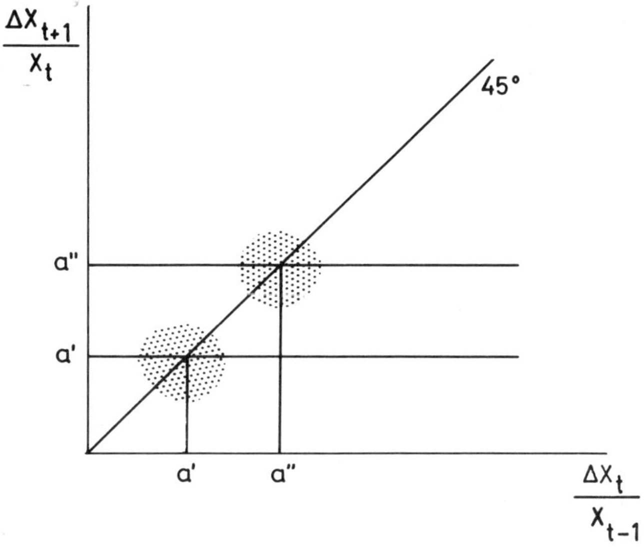

To examine whether this type of bias is present in the South Korean monthly series, autocorrelation functions were estimated for three segments of six, four and eight years, respectively. The autocorrelation coefficients are reported for up to lag 16 in Table 12. In the autocorrelation functions of the first and third segments, no coefficient is significant. But in the autocorrelation function of the second segment, two coefficients are significant at the five per cent level. A closer look at the second sub-period shows that the official exchange rate of won was devalued frequently in the years 1964-1965 [1]. This resulted in many discrete shifts in the mean of the process generating the rates of return on currency positions. These shifts could have biased the autocorrelation coefficients for the monthly South Korean series in favour of dependency. Hence, at least for the segmented series it could be concluded that the null hypothesis of mar-

[1] For instance, the won was devalued on 3rd May, 1964 and a system of fluctuating rate was introduced. It was further devalued in March and in June of 1965. When these two years are dropped from the second sub-period, the autocorrelation functions for the remaining two years turn out to be random.

Table 12 - Autocorrelation of the Segmented South Korean Monthly Series (219 Months)

Lag	January 1958 to December 1963	January 1964 to December 1967	January 1968 to March 1976
1	0.13	0.45*	0.19
2	0.16	0.43*	-0.14
3	0.11	0.23	-0.12
4	-0.21	0.00	0.00
5	0.08	0.09	-0.11
6	-0.07	0.05	0.01
7	0.07	0.09	-0.13
8	-0.07	0.05	-0.01
9	-0.16	-0.04	0.11
10	0.08	-0.04	0.05
11	-0.18	-0.04	-0.19
12	0.07	-0.17	-0.06
13	0.11	-0.14	-0.03
14	-0.27	-0.27	-0.15
15	0.08	-0.26	-0.13
16	-0.20	-0.15	0.21

*Significant at the 5 per cent level.

ket efficiency for the South Korean won cannot be rejected, though there are some signs of dependence in the pooled series.

Runs Analysis

This analysis has been widely used for testing the randomness of the series of stock prices [Fama, 1965] and freely floating exchange rates [Burt et al., 1977; Cornell, Dietrich, 1978].

A run is defined as a sequence of price changes of the same sign. Runs of +, - and 0 price changes for monthly and weekly exchange rate series of the three currencies were computed. The details of runs of different lengths of +, - and 0 are represented in Tables 13 through 15.

By assuming that the sample proportions of positive, negative and zero price changes are good estimates of the population proportions, under the hypothesis of independence, the total expected number of runs of all signs of an exchange rate series were estimated as follows[1]:

$$(27) \qquad m = \frac{\left[N\,(N+1) - \sum_{i=1}^{3} n_j^2 \right]}{N}$$

where N is the total number of price changes, and n the number of price changes of each sign. The standard error of m is

$$(28) \qquad \sigma_m = \left[\frac{\sum_{i=1}^{3} n_i^2 \left[\sum_{i=1}^{3} n_i^2 + N\,(N+1) \right] - 2N \sum_{i=1}^{3} n_i^3 - N^3}{N^2\,(N-1)} \right]^{\frac{1}{2}}$$

For large samples, the distribution of the total number of runs is approximately normal with mean m and standard er-

[1] This section relies heavily on Fama [1965, pp. 74-76].

Table 13 - Runs Analysis of Weekly and Monthly Series for India

Run Length in Weeks/ Months	Weekly Series			Monthly Series		
	observed					
	-	+	0	-	+	0
1	23	23	21	25	23	5
2	8	11	6	16	11	2
3	4	0	2	4	6	0
4	0	1	3	2	6	0
5	0	0	0	3	2	0
6	0	0	0	0	1	0
7	0	0	1	0	2	0
Total	35	35	33	50	51	7

Table 14 - Runs Analysis of Weekly and Monthly Series for South Korea

Run Length in Weeks/ Months	Weekly Series			Monthly Series		
	observed					
	-	+	0	-	+	0
1	29	25	20	22	19	11
2	3	1	6	8	6	2
3	0	1	7	8	8	2
4	0	0	3	1	7	1
5	0	0	1	1	1	0
6	0	0	0	0	0	0
7	0	0	1	1	0	0
8	0	0	2	0	1	0
9	.	.	.	0	1	0
10	.	.	.	1	0	0
Total	32	27	40	42	43	16

Table 15 - Runs Analysis of Weekly and Monthly Series for Taiwan

Run Length in Weeks/ Months	Weekly Series			Monthly Series		
	observed					
	-	+	0	-	+	0
1	29	28	16	30	21	4
2	9	8	2	18	24	0
3	5	3	1	4	3	1
4	1	1	0	2	6	0
5	0	1	0	1	1	0
6	0	0	0	1	0	0
7	0	0	0	1	0	0
Total	44	42	19	57	55	5

ror σ_m. To test whether the difference between the actual and the expected number of runs is significantly different, the following statistic is computed:

(29) $$K = \frac{(R + 1/2) - m}{\sigma_m}$$

where R is the actual number of runs, K is a standard normal variate distributed with mean zero and variance one, and 1/2 in the numerator is a discontinuity adjustment. If K lies in the interval +1.96 and -1.96, then the hypothesis of independence cannot be rejected at the five per cent level of significance.

The total expected and actual number of runs for the weekly and the monthly series are shown in Table 16. The results indicate that for the weekly series of all three currencies and the monthly series of the Indian rupee and the Taiwan dollar the difference between the observed and the expected number of runs is insignificant at the 5 per cent level.

However, the actual number of runs for the monthly South Korean won are less than the expected and this difference is significant at the five per cent level indicating positive

Table 16 - Currency Price Change Runs for Weekly and Monthly Series

Currency	Total Runs		Standard Error
	observed	expected	
		159 weeks	
Indian rupee	103	106.05	6.05
South Korean won	99	90.81	5.396
Taiwan dollar	105	97.95	5.99
		219 months	
Indian rupee	108	117.01	7.16
South Korean won	101	130.04	6.84*
Taiwan dollar	117	116.64	7.30

*Significant at the 5 per cent level.

serial correlation. But, this result is not unexpected given that these series are mean nonstationary. Therefore, the results of the runs analysis also tend to support the efficient market hypothesis.

Filter Rules

In order to detect dependencies that are not a strict function of time (e.g., are of nonlinear form), certain trading strategies called filter rules have been devised. These filter rules were first employed by Alexander [1961] to identify potentially profitable swings in stock prices.

The filters are buy-and-sell rules on past and current behaviour of the exchange rate. The rule employed in this study is, "Buy when the price is X per cent above its previous low and sell when price is Y per cent below its previous high." As is evident, an infinite number of such rules can be designed by varying X and Y and changing the basic form of the above mentioned rule[1]. The profits from following these trading rules should then be compared to the profits from buying and holding the currency. The latter does not refer to buying and holding the home currency but to buying the foreign currency in the beginning of the period and then selling it at the end of the period to get back into the domestic currency[2].

In applying these rules, the following assumptions are made:

(a) The trader does not engage in short selling and all transactions take place in the spot market.

(b) The investor has already made decisions with regard to the allocation of wealth among domestic securities and has available with him some cash balances. The filter rules only act as a guide in the allocation of these cash balances among different kinds of money.

(c) No interest is earned on any of the funds. In other words, there is no investment income, so that the reported profits accrue only from following the trading strategy and holding money.

(d) There are no transaction costs.

There is a serious limitation in the filter rule strategies. The application of these rules to stock markets have involved shifts between money and securities, that is, between two assets only, whereas the portfolio theory makes a strong case for a fully diversified portfolio consisting not only of money and securities but of different types of currencies, bonds etc. However, this limitation is generally accepted for the sake of simplicity and also because it is impossible to prove that no profits can be made under any rule.

To reduce the number of trading strategies to a manageable number, buy and sell filters (X per cent and Y per cent

---

[1] One such modification is the moving average rule. Under this rule, a moving average of a specified length is calculated and foreign currency purchased when the exchange rate moves X per cent above the moving average; when it falls Y per cent below the moving average, the investor moves back into the domestic currency.

[2] For a detailed rationale on this, see Logue and Sweeney [1977].

above) were assumed to be equal in all cases. These buy and sell limits vary between 0.25 and 4 per cent for the weekly series and between 0.25 and 8 per cent for the monthly series. The results from application of these rules are given in Tables 17 through 19.[1]

The results show that for weekly exchange rate series filters greater than 1 per cent yield negative rates of return for all three currencies. However, for filters between 0.25 and 0.75 per cent, positive annual rates of return were realized, some in excess of 10 per cent. For the monthly series, filters below 1 per cent generally outperformed the buy-and-hold strategy. However, two points should be kept in mind when interpreting some of these high rates of return:

- First, these rates of return are not net of transaction costs. These costs tend to be particularly high in a black market where the information on participants and prices is imperfect, and the market is relatively thin.
- Second, for our purposes, it is the average profit per transaction which is of relevance. Positive profits can be realized only when the transaction costs are less than the average profit per transaction.

Though a reliable estimate of the transaction costs is not available, some indication of these costs can be obtained by looking at the buy-and-sell differential reported in Table 20 for a typical day[2]. The buy-and-sell differential as a percentage of selling price varies between 3 to 8.33 per cent. Even if 3 per cent is the representative figure of transaction costs in these markets, all filter rule profits either disappear or turn out to be less than with the buy and hold strategy.

It was pointed out earlier that the profits reported in Tables 14 through 16, col. 4, are those resulting from following a trading strategy alone and are unadjusted for interest income.

---

[1] For a description of technical details relating to filter rules see the Appendix.

[2] This information has been provided by Deak and Co., Hongkong. The weekly black market exchange rate data published in the Far Eastern Economic Review name this agency as the source.

Table 17 - Application of Filter Rules to Weekly and Monthly Series for India

Filter Size	Average Number of Transaction per year	Before Transaction Costs	
		average profit per transaction	average profit per year
per cent		per cent	
		159 weeks	
4	1.96	-2.49	-4.83
3	2.94	-1.49	-4.32
2	5.23	-1.55	-7.84
1.5	5.23	-1.46	-7.38
1	7.52	-0.90	-6.54
0.75	7.52	-0.90	-6.54
0.5	8.83	0.55	4.96
0.25	8.83	0.55	4.96
Buy and hold			-2.016
		219 months	
8	0.66	2.80	1.83
6	0.88	1.81	1.59
5	1.10	1.62	1.78
4	1.15	2.16	2.49
3	1.20	3.05	3.60
2	1.25	2.80	3.50
1	1.92	3.36	6.54
0.5	2.30	2.55	5.96
0.25	2.58	2.48	6.52
Buy and hold			3.54

Table 18 - Application of Filter Rules to Weekly and Monthly Series for South Korea

Filter Size	Average Number of Transaction per year	Before Transaction Costs	
		average profit per transaction	average profit per year
per cent		per cent	
		159 weeks	
4	0.33	2.91	0.94
3	0.65	0.53	-0.34
2	1.64	-0.23	-0.37
1.5	1.96	-0.26	-0.52
1	3.27	-0.12	-0.40
0.75	5.56	-0.69	-3.76
0.5	6.21	-0.63	-3.85
0.25	6.87	-0.68	-4.60
Buy and hold			-0.637
		219 months	
8	0.44	17.57	7.35
6	0.53	14.70	7.54
5	0.60	12.02	7.05
4	0.88	8.80	7.68
3	1.04	7.18	7.49
2	1.10	6.70	7.39
1	1.53	5.86	9.13
0.5	1.92	4.14	8.09
0.25	2.08	4.14	8.82
Buy and hold			7.71

Table 19 - Application of Filter Rules to Weekly and Monthly Series for Taiwan

Filter Size	Average Number of Transaction per year	Before Transaction Costs	
		average profit per transaction	average profit per year
per cent		per cent	
		159 weeks	
4	1.96	-1.57	-3.05
3	2.62	-1.38	-3.56
2	3.60	-0.77	-2.73
1.5	4.58	-0.47	-2.11
1	6.54	-0.40	-2.58
0.75	7.19	0.35	2.54
0.5	10.21	0.94	10.02
0.25	11.45	1.01	12.19
Buy and hold			-3.104
		219 months	
8	0.44	0.22	0.10
6	0.49	0.39	0.19
5	0.55	0.68	0.37
4	0.77	0.10	0.07
3	1.10	-1.06	-1.16
2	1.48	-0.46	-0.68
1	2.14	-1.02	-2.17
0.5	2.74	-0.94	-2.57
0.25	2.90	-1.04	-2.99
Buy and hold			0.22

Table 20 - The Buy/Sell Rates for Rupee, Won and NT Dollar on March 3, 1980

Currency	Buying Price	Selling Price	Transaction Costs
	in Hongkong dollars for 100		per cent
Indian rupee	55.00	57.00	3.51
South Korean won	0.62	0.72	8.33
New Taiwan dollar	13.00	13.40	2.99

Source: Deak and Co., Hongkong.

If an interest differential exists in favour of the home country, then the filter profits (unadjusted for this interest differential) would tend to be biased in the upward direction[1].

In a developing country, usually controls also exist on the financial sector of the economy, These controls take the form of interest rate ceilings on deposits. This causes a black market for loanable funds to emerge in addition to a black market in foreign currencies. The interest rates in these markets are generally higher than those in the controlled market. If these high interest rates are used to adjust the profits from the various trading strategies, the corrected profits would be even lower. Thus, any claim that corre-

---

[1] The implicit assumption is that the money is held for half the period under consideration in the home currency and for the other half in the foreign currency. Thus, the interest earnings of the individuals using the filter strategy to exploit the profitable swings are smaller as compared with the earnings of those not following the filter strategy.
An indication of interest rate differentials between the United States and the other countries for the period covered by this study can be obtained by examining the short-term interest rates. For instance, in the United States, the short-term interest rate during 1958-1979 rose from 2.5 to 10.4 per cent. For South Korea and India, it rose from 6.6 to 15 per cent, and from 4 to 8.5 per cent, respectively. For Taiwan, it fell from 14.4 to 12.5 per cent [International Financial Statistics].

lates high (unadjusted) profits with market inefficiency must be viewed with scepticism.

Finally, all users of filter rule strategies must realize that filter rules are constructed ex post, whereas the real test of market efficiency ought to be based on ex ante rules. Poole [1967, p. 477] pointed out that, "It is obvious that for any particular series ... one could always construct, ex post, some mechanical trading rule which would have provided excellent returns. A test of a mechanical trading rule requires that the rule be selected first and the series later."

Cross-Correlations

Finally, cross-correlations between ΔXb_t and ΔXo_t were estimated for each country for both the weekly and the monthly exchange rate series[1]. Cross-correlations, $R(\Delta Xb_t, \Delta Xo_{t+k})$ for lags 0 to 16 for the weekly and the monthly series were computed. These are reported in Table 21. The statistical significance of non-negative lags was examined to see if the movements in the official rate are "predicted" (or anticipated) by the black market rates.

In only three instances for the weekly series were the coefficients significant at the 5 per cent level. These were for the zero-week and one-week lags for South Korea and for the nine-week lag for Taiwan. However, the latter was barely significant. These results indicate that for South Korea the black market anticipated changes in the weekly official exchange rate one week ahead and for Taiwan possibly nine weeks ahead. For India, it seems that changes in the weekly black market exchange rates are poor short-term "predictors" of changes in the official exchange rate.

In the monthly series, seven coefficients were found to be statistically significant. These were for lags zero and three for South Korea, lag zero for India, and lags zero, four,

---

[1] Since Taiwan had a system of multiple (official) exchange rates up to June, 1960, the monthly period for this country ranges from July, 1960 to March, 1976.

Table 21 - Cross-Correlations Between Official and Black Market Exchange Rates for India, South Korea and Taiwan

Lag	India		South Korea		Taiwan	
	weekly	monthly	weekly	monthly	weekly	monthly
	coefficients					
0	0.09	0.16*	0.46*	0.27*	0.00	0.14*
1	-0.04	0.03	-0.30*	0.00	-0.01	-0.02
2	-0.01	0.05	0.00	-0.03	-0.08	0.03
3	-0.08	0.07	0.04	0.15*	0.06	0.13
4	0.04	0.02	0.02	-0.02	-0.02	-0.17*
5	-0.03	0.05	-0.03	-0.02	0.08	-0.06
6	0.01	0.00	0.01	0.00	-0.05	-0.02
7	0.01	0.12	-0.01	-0.04	-0.07	0.01
8	-0.02	-0.04	0.00	0.05	0.06	0.09
9	0.03	-0.10	-0.02	0.10	-0.16*	0.04
10	0.01	-0.10	0.03	0.05	0.03	0.04
11	0.02	0.04	-0.03	0.04	-0.03	0.09
12	-0.03	0.09	0.03	0.03	0.01	0.01
13	0.01	0.12	-0.01	0.03	0.15	0.27*
14	-0.06	-0.04	0.00	-0.02	-0.15	-0.28*
15	-0.05	0.04	0.00	-0.01	-0.02	-0.14
16	-0.13	0.03	0.00	0.08	0.09	0.03

*Significant at the 5 per cent level.

thirteen and fourteen for Taiwan. The highly significant coefficients at lag zero for all three countries suggest that the black market rate responds immediately to changes in the official rate. The significance at lags other than zero for South Korea and Taiwan suggests that changes in the official rate are, in large part, anticipated in these countries. In South Korea, for instance, the black market anticipates changes in the official rate three months before. In Taiwan, on the other hand, changes in the official rate seem to be anticipated as much as thirteen months ahead. Thus, the black market exchange rates anticipate changes in the official exchange rate in South Korea and Taiwan, but not in the case of India.

5. Conclusions

In this chapter, models of the weak-form version of the efficient market hypothesis with reference to the exchange rates were discussed. One such model was used to test whether the foreign exchange trading in the black market in India, South Korea and Taiwan is efficient or not.

Black markets are characterized by high transaction costs and imperfect information regarding prices and participants. Further, these markets are often thin and segmented. All these factors are potential impediments to an efficient adjustment of exchange rates to any new information. The purpose of this chapter was to see whether these impediments are strong enough to cause market inefficiency.

The tests of market efficiency consisted of statistical significance of autocorrelation coefficients of rates of return on currency positions, runs analysis and Alexanderian filter rules. Only the filter rules provided some evidence of market inefficiency when the filters chosen were less than 1 percent. But, when account is taken of the transaction costs, it becomes difficult to reject the hypothesis that black markets in foreign currencies in India, South Korea and Taiwan are efficient at least in the weak-form sense. These conclusions are similar to those arrived at by Giddy [1978a] for Israel, Peru and Brazil and Fishelson [1978] for Israel.

The estimates of cross-correlations between black market and official exchange rates suggest that for South Korea and Taiwan movements in the official rate are "predicted" (or anticipated) by the black market exchange rates. However, in India the black market exchange rate is not an efficient indicator of official exchange rate changes[1]. The significance of cross-correlations between the black market and the official exchange rates could also mean that the policy makers in South Korea and Taiwan use the black market rate as a guide for setting the official exchange rate.

---

[1] Giddy [1978a] found that for Israel, Peru and Brazil, the weekly black market exchange rates were poor predictors of the official exchange rate. But for the monthly series, he found [1978b] black market exchange rates to possess significant predictive power.

V. Concluding Comments

Black markets in foreign currencies usually emerge whenever restrictions are imposed on the foreign sector of an economy. In this study, I examined the nature of these markets, the determinants of the black market exchange rate for India and the efficiency of black markets in foreign exchange in India, South Korea and Taiwan.

I showed in Chapter I, first, that the determinants of black markets in foreign currencies are of great interest to the central bank of a country, for the black market exchange rate affects the reserve flows. A differential between the official and the black market exchange rate tends to create an incentive for traders to under- and over-invoice exports and imports, thus diverting foreign exchange transactions to the black market. Second, a premium on foreign currencies also diverts the flow of remittances to this market by residents abroad. Third, the practice of under- and over-invoicing distorts the composition of the official trade figures, thereby affecting the aid flows and hence the stock of reserves.

The survey of empirical estimates in Chapter II indicates that the under-invoicing of exports and imports has formed a significant proportion of the official exports and imports, respectively. This in turn reflects the fact that the tariff/subsidy structure in India has been such that an incentive is created to under-invoice exports and imports in the presence of controls on the foreign exchange market. The severity of the restrictions on foreign trade was further evidenced by the fact that smuggling as a proportion of official imports was as high as 10 per cent, at times even higher. This also points to the large losses in government revenue which could have been used to provide public goods.

In the light of numerous shortcomings of the existing models, I attempted to rebuild the model for the determinants of the exchange rate in the black market in Chapter III. The model was oriented so as to incorporate the features peculiar to the Indian economy. In developing the model, some of the important assumptions associated with the monetary approach to exchange rate determination were reformulated. The black market exchange rate was determined by the conditions of stock equilibrium rather than by the current flow demands and supplies of foreign exchange. Further, the relationship of the black market exchange rate with smuggling was explicitly taken into account. The reduced-form expression obtained showed that the principal determinants of the exchange rate in the black market for India are the official exchange rate, the nominal quantity of money, the real level of income, the interest rate, the world prices of gold and silver and the world price level. The parameters of this model were estimated by using ordinary least squares. The results showed that changes in the domestic money stock, the interest rate, the world price of gold and the domestic real income have a statistically significant effect on the black market exchange rate.

In a country where the official exchange rate is overvalued but pegged and the foreign exchange is allocated by the authorities, the official foreign exchange reserves fluctuate indirectly as a result of monetary disequilibrium at home. As the statistical results presented in Chapter III indicate, an increase in the domestic money stock results in a depreciation of the black market exchange rate. This increases the discrepancy between the official and the black market exchange rate, thereby increasing the incentive to under-invoice exports and lowering the incentive to over-invoice exports. Further, rising domestic prices cause exporters to divert exports to the domestic market. Thus, one arrives at the familiar result that under fixed exchange rates an expansion of the domestic credit component results in a loss of foreign exchange reserves [Johnson, 1973]. Therefore, a restraint on the domestic credit creation is one of the important options available to the central bank for preventing reserve losses when there exists a black market for foreign currencies.

The results further suggest that the price of gold in the world market greatly influences the price of one U. S. dollar in the black market. The rising world price of gold through increased money demand tends to lower (appreciate) the black market exchange rate. Hence, if legal import of gold is allowed freely, the resulting loss of foreign exchange may not be considered "desirable," especially when this foreign exchange is required for other higher valued alternatives (primarily, for development). But, it is well-known that smuggling is not always welfare maximizing[1] and smuggling of gold coupled with exchange controls contributes to the emergence of a black market, which indirectly affects reserves in the way discussed earlier in the first chapter. To all this should then be added the cost of enforcement. Therefore, the "optimum" policy appears to be to balance the loss of reserves due to legally permitted imports of gold against the increased flow of reserves which would result from the reduced size of the black market (and a lower premium on the foreign currencies in this market).

Further, as the empirical results in Chapter III were generally supportive of the model, it shows the richness of the monetary approach to the exchange rate determination. By reformulating some of the main assumptions, interesting results were obtained for the black market exchange rate.

Weak-form tests of market efficiency were performed on the black market exchange rate series for India, South Korea and Taiwan in Chapter IV. I carried out these tests on both the weekly and the monthly exchange rate series. The tests consisted of the statistical significance of autocorrelation functions of rates of return, nonparametric tests like the runs analysis and Alexanderian filter rules. Some evidence of market inefficiency was found in the use of filters less than 1 per cent. However, when account is taken of the transaction costs these profits are no greater than those found for a buy and hold strategy. Thus, the overall results suggested that it is difficult to reject the hypothesis that black markets in foreign currencies in India, South Korea and Taiwan are efficient at least in the weak-form sense. In this context, the predictive power of black market exchange rates was evaluated by examining the significance of the cross-correlation coefficients between changes in the official and the black market exchange rates. The results indicated that changes in the black market exchange rate were poor "predictors" of changes in the official rate in the case of India. However, relatively good "predictions" were obtained for South Korea and Taiwan, particularly for the monthly official exchange rate series.

---

[1] For a detailed welfare analysis of smuggling, see Bhagwati and Hansen [1973], and Johnson [1974].

The importance of this study on the efficiency of a black market arises from the fact that it provides more evidence on the efficiency of financial markets generally, and specifically for one which does not appear to possess all the characteristics assumed to be necessary for efficiency. The results could also be used by the policy makers interested in employing black market exchange rates to study the market trends and for determining the official exchange rates.

Appendix

1. Data Sources for Chapter III

Eb = Price of one U. S. dollar in rupees in the black market, quarterly average of the monthly data [Pick's Currency Yearbook, 1975-76].

Eo = Price of one U. S. dollar in rupees in the official market, quarterly average of the monthly data [IMF, International Financial Statistics].

M = Stock of M1 in India, quarterly average of the monthly data, seasonally adjusted [IMF, International Financial Statistics].

i = Interest rate in India, proxied by the quarterly average of monthly call money rate [IMF, International Financial Statistics].

Pg' = Price of gold in the world market, approximated by the quarterly average of monthly prices in the London gold market [Bank of England, Quarterly Bulletin].

Ps' = Price of silver in the world market, quarterly average of the monthly prices in New York, where the monthly price has been approximated by taking the average of prices in the middle of the month and at the end of month (for daily prices [Wall Street Journal]).

Pw = Price level in the rest of the world, proxied by the U. S. implicit price deflator, obtained by dividing nominal GNP by real GNP (1972, $), and then multiplying by 100 [Survey of Current Business, January 1976; July 1977, Table 1.2].

Yp = Real income in India, approximated by the quarterly average of monthly index of industrial production, seasonally adjusted [IMF, International Financial Statistics; Monthly Abstract of Statistics, Central Statistical Organisation, Government of India].

2. Description of Filter Rules

In this section, I discuss some technical details relating to the computation of the annual average filter profit.

The average profit per transaction, before commission, is estimated as follows[1] (in per cent):

For each move, as defined by a specified filter, let the variable M denote the difference between the logarithms of the upper and the lower endpoints of a move, which represent the peak and the trough prices, respectively. The average of all moves (M) is computed and $\bar{R}$, the average logarithmic profit, is then defined as $\bar{R} = \bar{M} - 2F - 2b$, where F is $\log_{10}(1 + f)$ and f is the filter expressed as 0.10 for a 10 per cent filter, and $2\bar{b}$ represents the average logarithmic difference between the closing prices and the triggering prices of the days the triggering prices were crossed. The quantity 2F refers to the portion of the move that is used up in getting in and out. Here, it should be noted that R is also the difference between the average closing selling and buying prices.

If a transactor is not allowed to short-sell, then it is possible for him to make profits only on the upmoves so that in this case M would be the difference between the trough and the peak prices. On an upmove of average size M, the percentage profit would be Pu = 100 (antilog R-1). If short-selling is assumed, then M would be redefined as the difference between a trough and a peak, and a peak and a trough. The re-estimated $\bar{M}$ would then be used to compute P_u and also percentage profit on a downmove, Pd = 100 Pu/(100 + Pu).

The average profit when short-selling is permitted is estimated as:

$$P = (100 + Pu)^{\frac{1}{2}} (100 + Pd)^{\frac{1}{2}} - 100$$

[1] This section relies on Alexander [1961; 1964].

The average number of annual transactions: A transaction is defined as a purchase and sale, thus requiring two commissions. For each exchange rate series, there is one terminal transaction, terminated not by a filter signal but by the period limit. The corresponding terminal move is counted as half a move in the computation of M, and the number of transactions per year.

The annual average profit, before commission, is estimated as follows (in per cent):

$$100\,[1 + (P/100)]^{q} - 100$$

where q is the average number of transactions per year. However, when short-selling is not assumed, then P above is replaced by P_u.

References

Alexander, Sidney S., "Price Movements in Speculative Markets: Trading or Random Walks." Industrial Management Review, Vol. 2, Cambridge, Mass., 1961, pp. 7-26.

--, "Price Movements in Speculative Markets: Trends or Random Walks, No. 2." Ibid., Vol. 5, 1964, pp. 24-46.

Becker, Gary S., William M. Landes, Essays in the Economics of Crime and Punishment. National Bureau of Economic Research, New York, 1974.

Bhagwati, Jagdish N., "On the Under-invoicing of Imports." Bulletin of the Oxford University Institute of Economics and Statistics, Vol. 26, Oxford, 1964, pp. 389-393.

--, "Fiscal Policies, the Faking of Foreign Trade Declarations, and the Balance of Payments." Ibid., Vol. 29, 1967, pp. 61-77.

-- (Ed.), Illegal Transactions in International Trade: Theory and Measurement. Studies in International Economics, Vol. 1, Amsterdam, 1974.

--, Bent Hansen, "A Theoretical Analysis of Smuggling." The Quarterly Journal of Economics, Vol. 87, Cambridge, Mass., 1973, pp. 172-187.

Bilson, John F.O., "Rational Expectations and the Exchange Rate." In: Jacob A. Frenkel, Harry G. Johnson (Eds.), Economics of Exchange Rates: Selected Studies. Addison-Wesley Series in Economics, Reading, 1978, pp. 75-96.

Blejer, Mario I., "Exchange Restrictions and the Monetary Approach to the Exchange Rate." In: Jacob A. Frenkel, Harry G. Johnson (Eds.), The Economics of Exchange Rates: Selected Studies. Addison-Wesley Series in Economics, Reading, 1978, pp. 117-128.

Boorman, John T., "The Evidence on the Demand for Money: Theoretical Formulations and Empirical Results." In: Thomas M. Havrilesky, John T. Boorman (Eds.), Current Issues in Monetary Theory and Policy. Arlington Heights, 1976, pp. 315-361.

Boulding, Kenneth E., "A Note on the Theory of the Black Market." The Canadian Journal of Economics and Political Science, Vol. 13, Toronto, 1947, pp. 115-118.

Box, George E. P., Gwilym Jenkins, Time Series Analysis: Forecasting and Control. San Francisco, 1976.

Branson, William H., Macroeconomic Theory and Policy. 2nd Ed., New York, 1979.

Bronfenbrenner, Martin, "Price Control Under Perfect Competition." The American Economic Review, Vol. 37, Evanston, 1947, pp. 107-120.

Burt, John, Fred R. Kaen, G. Geoffrey Booth, "Foreign Exchange Market Efficiency Under Flexible Exchange Rates." Journal of Finance, Vol. 32, Worcester, Mass., 1977, pp. 1325-1330.

--, --, --, "Foreign Exchange Market Efficiency Under Flexible Exchange Rates: A Reply." Ibid., Vol. 34, Worcester, Mass., 1979, pp. 791-793.

Chow, Gregory, "On the Long-Run and Short-Run Demand for Money." Journal of Political Economy, Vol. 74, Chicago, 1966, pp. 111-131.

Cohen, Jerome B., Japan's Economy in War and Reconstruction. Minneapolis, 1949.

Connolly, Michael, José D.A. Silveira, "Exchange Market Pressure in Postwar Brazil: An Application of the Girton-Roper Monetary Model." The American Economic Review, Vol. 69, Menasha, 1979, pp. 448-454.

Cooper, Richard N., "Tariffs and Smuggling in Indonesia." In: Jagdish N. Bhagwati (Ed.), Illegal Transactions in International Trade: Theory and Measurement. Amsterdam, 1974.

Cootner, Paul H. (Ed.), The Random Character of Stock Market Prices. Cambridge, Mass., 1964.

Cornell, W. Bradford, J. Kimball Dietrich, "The Efficiency of the Market for Foreign Exchange Under Floating Exchange Rates." Review of Economics and Statistics, Vol. 60, Cambridge, Mass., 1978, pp. 111-120.

Culbertson, Jr., William P., "Purchasing Power Parity and Black Market Exchange Rates." Economic Inquiry, Vol. 13, Long Beach, 1975, pp. 287-296.

Culbertson, Jr., Ryan C. Amacher, "Inflation in the Planned Economies: Some Estimates for Eastern Europe." Southern Economic Journal, Vol. 45, Chapel Hill, 1978, pp. 380-393.

Dornbusch, Rudiger [1976a], "The Theory of Flexible Exchange Rate Regimes and Macroeconomic Policy." The Scandinavian Journal of Economics, Vol. 78, Stockholm, 1976, pp. 253-275.

-- [1976b], "Expectations and Exchange Rate Dynamics." Journal of Political Economy, Vol. 84, Chicago, 1976, pp. 1161-1176.

Fama, Eugene F., "The Behavior of Stock-Market Prices." Journal of Business, Vol. 38, Chicago, 1965, pp. 34-105.

--, "Efficient Capital Markets: A Review of Theory and Empirical Work." Journal of Finance, Vol. 25, Worcester, Mass., 1970, pp. 383-417.

--, Foundations of Finance. New York, 1976.

--, Lawrence Fisher, Michael C. Jensen, Richard Roll, "The Adjustment of Stock Prices to New Information." International Economic Review, Vol. 10, Osaka, 1969, pp. 1-21.

Far Eastern Economic Review, Hongkong, various issues.

Fishelson, Gideon, "The Determinants of Black Market Exchange Rates." The Foerder Institute for Economic Research, Tel-Aviv University, Working Paper No. 32/76, 1978.

Frenkel, Jacob A., "A Monetary Approach to the Exchange Rate: Doctrinal Aspects and Empirical Evidence." Scandinavian Journal of Economics, Vol. 78, Stockholm, 1976, pp. 200-224.

--, Richard M. Levich, "Covered Interest Arbitrage: Unexplained Profits." Journal of Political Economy, Vol. 83, Chicago, 1975, pp. 325-338.

Friedman, Milton, "The Quantity Theory of Money: A Restatement." In: Milton Friedman (Ed.), Studies in the Quantity Theory of Money. Studies in Economics of the Economics Research Center of the University of Chicago, Chicago, 1956.

Giddy, Ian H. [1978a], "The Efficiency of Black Markets for Foreign Exchange." A Paper Presented at the Academy of International Business Annual Meetings, Chicago, 1978.

-- [1978b], "The Predictive Power of Black Market Exchange Rates." Business International Money Report, June 1978, pp. 186-187.

--, Gunter Dufey, "The Random Behaviour of Flexible Exchange Rates: Implications for Forecasting." Journal of International Business, Vol. 6, Atlanta, 1975, pp. 1-32.

Girton, Lance, Don Roper, "A Monetary Model of Exchange Market Pressure Applied to the Postwar Canadian Experience." The American Economic Review, Vol. 67, Menasha, 1977, pp. 537-548.

Goodman, Stephen H., "Foreign Exchange Rate Forecasting Techniques: Implications for Business and Policy." Journal of Finance, Vol. 34, Worcester, Mass., 1979, pp. 415-427.

Granger, C. W. J., O. Morgenstern, The Predictability of Stock Market Prices. Boston, 1970.

Grubel, Herbert G., International Economics. Homewood, 1977.

Harberger, Arnold C. (Ed.), The Demand for Durable Goods. Studies in Economics of the Economics Research Center of the University of Chicago, Chicago, 1960.

Hirshleifer, Jack, Price Theory and Applications. Englewood Cliffs, 1976.

Hodrick, Robert J., "An Empirical Analysis of the Monetary Approach to the Determination of the Exchange Rate." In: Jacob A. Frenkel, Harry G. Johnson (Eds.), Economics of Exchange Rates: Selected Studies. Addison-Wesley Series in Economics, Reading, 1978, pp. 97-116.

International Monetary Fund, International Financial Statistics, Washington, various issues.

Johnson, Harry G., "The Monetary Approach to Balance of Payments Theory." In: Michael B. Connolly, Alexander K. Swoboda (Eds.), International Trade and Money. London, 1973, pp. 206-224.

Johnson, Harry G., "Notes on the Economic Theory of Smuggling." In: Jagdish N. Bhagwati (Ed.), Illegal Transactions in International Trade: Theory and Measurement. Amsterdam, 1974, pp. 39-46.

Johnston, Jack, Econometric Methods. 2nd Ed., New York, 1972.

Kaul Committee Report, Report of the Study Team on Leakage of Foreign Exchange Through Invoice Manipulation. Ministry of Finance, Government of India, New Delhi, 1971.

Klein, Benjamin, "Competitive Interest Payments on Bank Deposits and the Long-Run Demand for Money." The American Economic Review, Vol. 64, Menasha, 1974, pp. 931-949.

Krugman, Paul K., "Purchasing Power Parity and Exchange Rates, Another Look at the Evidence." Journal of International Economics, Vol. 8, Amsterdam, 1978, pp. 397-407.

Laidler, David E. W., The Demand for Money: Theories and Evidence. International Series in Monetary Economics, Scranton, 1969.

Layard, P. R. G., A. A. Walters, Microeconomic Theory. New York, 1978.

Levich, Richard M., "On the Efficiency of Markets for Foreign Exchange." Paper Prepared for the Wingspread III Conference on "International Economic Policy: An Assessment of Theory and Evidence," July 27-30, 1977, Racine, Wis.

--, "Tests of Forecasting Models and Market Efficiency in the International Money Market." In: Jacob A. Frenkel and Harry G. Johnson (Eds.), Economics of Exchange Rates: Selected Studies. Addison-Wesley Series in Economics, Reading, 1978, pp. 129-158.

Lipschitz, Leslie, Ichiro Otani, "A Simple Model of the Private Gold Market, 1968-74: An Exploratory Econometric Exercise." IMF, Staff Papers, Vol. 24, Washington, 1977, pp. 36-66.

Little, Ian, Tibor Scitovsky, Maurice Scott, Industry and Trade in Some Developing Countries: A Comparative Study. London, 1970.

Loque, D.E., R.J. Sweeney, "White Noise in Imperfect Markets: The Case of the Franc/Dollar Exchange Rate." Journal of Finance, Vol. 32, Worcester, Mass., 1977, pp. 761-768.

--, --, Thomas D. Willet, "Speculative Behavior of Foreign Exchange Rates During the Current Float." Journal of Business Research, Vol. 6, Athens, Ga., 1978, pp. 159-174.

Maddala, G.S., Econometrics. New York, 1977.

Michaely, Michael, "A Geometrical Analysis of Black Market Behavior." The American Economic Review, Vol. 44, Evanston, 1954, pp. 627-637.

Miles, Marc A., D. Sykes Wilford, "Foreign Exchange Market Efficiency Under Flexible Exchange Rates: Comment." Journal of Finance, Vol. 34, Worcester, Mass., 1979, pp. 787-789.

Monthly Abstract of Statistics, Central Statistical Organisation of India, Department of Statistics, Ministry of Planning, Government of India, New Delhi, various issues.

Naya, Seiji, Theodore Morgan, "The Accuracy of International Trade Data: The Case of Southeast Asian Countries." In: Jagdish N. Bhagwati (Ed.), Illegal Transactions in International Trade: Theory and Measurement. Studies in International Economics, Vol. 1, Amsterdam, 1974, pp. 123-137.

Nayak, Satyendra S., "Illegal Transactions in External Trade and Payments in India: An Empirical Study." Economic and Political Weekly, Vol. 12, Bombay, 1977, pp. 2051-2062.

--, "Illegal Transactions in Trade and Payments in India: A Reply." Ibid., Vol. 14, 1979, pp. 39-40.

Nelson, Charles R., Applied Time Series Analysis. San Francisco, 1973.

Patinkin, Don, Money, Interest and Prices: An Integration of Monetary and Value Theory. 2nd Ed., New York, 1965.

Pick's Currency Yearbook, New York, 1967-1976.

Pindyck, R.S., D.L. Rubinfeld, Econometric Models and Economic Forecasts. New York, 1976.

Pippenger, John E., "The Case for Freely Fluctuating Exchange Rates: Some Evidence." Western Economic Journal, Vol. 11, Salt Lake City, 1973, pp. 314-326.

Pitre, Vidya, "Illegal Transactions in Trade and Payments: A Comment." Economic and Political Weekly, Vol. 13, Bombay, 1978, pp. 1154-1156.

Poole, William, "Speculative Prices as Random Walks - An Analysis of Ten Time Series of Flexible Exchange Rates." Southern Economic Journal, Vol. 33, Chapel Hill, 1967, pp. 468-478.

Prakash, B.A., "Impact of Foreign Remittances: A Case Study of Chavakkad Village in Kerala." Economic and Political Weekly, Vol. 13, Bombay, 1978, pp. 1107-1111.

Richter, H.V., "Problems of Assessing Unrecorded Trade." Bulletin of Indonesian Economic Studies, Vol. 6, Canberra, 1970, pp. 17-44.

Samuelson, Paul A., Foundations of Economic Analysis. Harvard Economic Studies, Vol. 80, Cambridge, Mass., 1948.

Sargen, Nicholas P., "Exchange Rate Flexibility and Demand for Money." Journal of Finance, Vol. 32, Worcester, Mass., 1977, pp. 531-544.

Sheikh, Munir A., "Black Market for Foreign Exchange, Capital Flows and Smuggling." Journal of Development Studies, Vol. 3, Amsterdam, 1976, pp. 9-26.

The Silver Market, 1977. 62nd Annual Review, New York.

Simkin, C.G.F., "Indonesia's Unrecorded Trade." Bulletin of Indonesian Studies, Vol. 6, Canberra, 1970, pp. 17-44.

Sweeney, R.S., "The Efficient Information Processing in Output Markets: Tests and Implications." Economic Inquiry, Vol. 16, Long Beach, 1978, pp. 313-333.

Tullio, Giuseppe, "The Fluctuations of the Price of Italian Banknotes in Zurich: An Econometric Analysis, February 1973-December 1975." Kyklos, Vol. 31, Basel, 1978, pp. 462-473.

White, Peter T., James L. Stanfield, "The Eternal Treasure Gold." National Geographic, Vol. 145, Washington, 1974, pp. 1-51.

Winston, Gordon C., "Overinvoicing, Underutilisation and Distorted Industrial Growth." Pakistan Development Review, Vol. 9, Karachi, 1969, pp. 405-421.

Kieler Studien

Institut für Weltwirtschaft an der Universität Kiel

Herausgegeben von Herbert Giersch
Schriftleitung: Hubertus Müller-Groeling

150. Stefan Baron, Hans H. Glismann, Bernd Stecher, Internationale Rohstoffpolitik. Ziele, Mittel, Kosten. 1977. XI, 194 S. Broschiert *DM* 28,–. Leinen *DM* 46,–.
151. Rolf J. Langhammer, Die Zentralafrikanische Zoll- und Wirtschaftsunion. Integrationswirkungen bei Ländern im Frühstadium der industriellen Entwicklung. 1978. XV, 268 S. Broschiert *DM* 50,–. Leinen *DM* 60,–.
152. Hugo Dicke, Strukturwandel im westdeutschen Straßenfahrzeugbau 1978. XI, 171 S. Broschiert *DM* 36,–. Leinen *DM* 48,–.
153. Jan Peter Wogart, Industrialization in Colombia: Policies, Patterns, Perspectives. 1978. XIII, 176 S. Broschiert *DM* 35,–. Leinen *DM* 49,–.
154. Sighart Nehring, Die Wirkungen von Handelspräferenzen im Warenaustausch zwischen der Bundesrepublik und der DDR. Ein empirischer Beitrag zur Theorie der impliziten Transfers. 1978. VII, 174 S. Broschiert *DM* 36,–. Leinen *DM* 48,–.
155. Frank Dietmar Weiss, Electrical Engineering in West Germany: Adjusting to Imports from Less Developed Countries. 1978. XII, 115 S. Broschiert *DM* 28,–. Leinen *DM* 40,–.
156. Roland Vaubel, Strategies for Currency Unification. The Economics of Currency Competition and the Case for a European Parallel Currency. 1978. XV, 471 S. Broschiert *DM* 74,–. Leinen *DM* 89,–.
157. Juergen B. Donges, Lotte Müller-Ohlsen, Außenwirtschaftsstrategien und Industrialisierung in Entwicklungsländern. 1978. IX, 239 S. Broschiert *DM* 44,–. Leinen *DM* 56,–.
158. Bernhard Heitger, Strukturelle Anpassungsprobleme der westdeutschen Metallverarbeitung. 1979. XII, 106 S. Broschiert *DM* 31,–. Leinen *DM* 43,–.
159. Rolf J. Langhammer, Die Bundesrepublik als Exportmarkt Lateinamerikas. Eine handelspolitische Analyse. 1979. XI, 163 S. Broschiert *DM* 38,–. Leinen *DM* 54,–.
160. Paulgeorg Juhl, Deutsche Direktinvestitionen in Lateinamerika. 1979. IX, 107 S. Broschiert *DM* 29,—. Leinen *DM* 43,–.
161. Richard W. T. Pomfret, Benjamin Toren, Israel and the European Common Market. An Appraisal of the 1975 Free Trade Agreement. 1980. XI, 204 S. Broschiert *DM* 49,–. Leinen *DM* 68,–.
162. Harmen Lehment, Devisenmarktinterventionen bei flexiblen Wechselkursen. Die Politik des Managed Floating. 1980. XIII, 289 S. Broschiert *DM* 57,–. Leinen *DM* 73,–.
163. Egbert Gerken, Arbeitsmärkte in Entwicklungsländern. 1981. XIV, 185 S. Broschiert *DM* 52,–. Leinen *DM* 70,–.
164. Horst Rodemer, Die EG-Agrarpolitik. Ziele, Wirkungen, Alternativen. 1980. XIII, 286 S. Broschiert *DM* 59,–. Leinen *DM* 77,–.
165. Lotte Müller-Ohlsen, Die Weltmetallwirtschaft im industriellen Entwicklungsprozeß. 1981. XI, 265 S. Broschiert *DM* 58,–. Leinen *DM* 76,–.
166. Gerhard Fels, Klaus-Dieter Schmidt und Mitarbeiter, Die deutsche Wirtschaft im Strukturwandel. 1981. XXII, 368 S. Broschiert *DM* 58,–. Leinen *DM* 76,–.
167. Sanjeev Gupta, Black Market Exchange Rates. 1981. XI, 100 S. Broschiert *DM* 31,–. Leinen *DM* 49,–.

J. C. B. Mohr (Paul Siebeck) Tübingen
Postfach 2040, D-7400 Tübingen
ISSN 0340 - 6989